New York Weekly Tests
- NYS ELA Format -

Grade 5

HOUGHTON MIFFLIN HARCOURT

Copyright © by Houghton Mifflin Harcourt Publishing Company

All rights reserved. No part of this work may be reproduced or transmitted in any form or by any means, electronic or mechanical, including photocopying or recording, or by any information storage or retrieval system, without the prior written permission of the copyright owner unless such copying is expressly permitted by federal copyright law.

Permission is hereby granted to individuals using the corresponding student's textbook or kit as the major vehicle for regular classroom instruction to photocopy entire pages from this publication in classroom quantities for instructional use and not for resale. Requests for information on other matters regarding duplication of this work should be addressed to Houghton Mifflin Harcourt Publishing Company, Attn: Contracts, Copyrights, and Licensing, 9400 South Park Center Loop, Orlando, Florida 32819.

Printed in the U.S.A.

ISBN-13: 978-0-547-40780-7
ISBN-10: 0-547-40780-7
4500260735
1 2 3 4 5 6 7 8 9 10 0930 18 17 16 15 14 13 12 11 10

If you have received these materials as examination copies free of charge, Houghton Mifflin Harcourt Publishing Company retains title to the materials and they may not be resold. Resale of examination copies is strictly prohibited.

Possession of this publication in print format does not entitle users to convert this publication, or any portion of it, into electronic format.

Contents

Unit 1 School Spirit! **1.1–5.10**
    Lesson 1: A Package for Mrs. Jewls 1.1–1.9
    Lesson 2: Ultimate Field Trip 5: Blasting Off to
              Space Academy 2.1–2.9
    Lesson 3: Off and Running 3.1–3.14
    Lesson 4: Double Dutch: A Celebration
              of Jump Rope, Rhyme, and Sisterhood 4.1–4.9
    Lesson 5: Elisa's Diary 5.1–5.10

Unit 2 Wild Encounters **6.1–10.10**
    Lesson 6: Interrupted Journey 6.1–6.10
    Lesson 7: Old Yeller 7.1–7.11
    Lesson 8: Everglades Forever 8.1–8.14
    Lesson 9: Storm Warriors 9.1–9.11
    Lesson 10: Cougars 10.1–10.10

Unit 3 Revolution! **11.1–15.10**
    Lesson 11: Dangerous Crossing 11.1–11.10
    Lesson 12: Can't You Make Them Behave, King George? 12.1–12.10
    Lesson 13: They Called Her Molly Pitcher 13.1–13.16
    Lesson 14: James Forten 14.1–14.9
    Lesson 15: We Were There, Too! 15.1–15.10

Unit 4 What's Your Story? **16.1–20.9**
    Lesson 16: Lunch Money 16.1–16.10
    Lesson 17: LAFFF 17.1–17.10
    Lesson 18: The Dog Newspaper 18.1–18.14
    Lesson 19: Darnell Rock Reporting 19.1–19.9
    Lesson 20: Don Quixote and the Windmills 20.1–20.9

Unit 5 Under Western Skies **21.1–25.10**
    Lesson 21: Tucket's Travels 21.1–21.10
    Lesson 22: The Birchbark House 22.1–22.10
    Lesson 23: Vaqueros: America's First Cowboys 23.1–23.14
    Lesson 24: Rachel's Journal 24.1–24.9
    Lesson 25: Lewis and Clark 25.1–25.10

Unit 6 Journey to Discovery **26.1–30.11**
    Lesson 26: Animals on the Move.. 26.1–26.9
    Lesson 27: Mysteries at Cliff Palace 27.1–27.9
    Lesson 28: Fossils: A Peak into the Past............................... 28.1–28.14
    Lesson 29: The Case of the Missing Deer 29.1–29.9
    Lesson 30: Get Lost! The Puzzle of the Mazes 30.1–30.11

Name _____ Date _____

Lesson 1
WEEKLY TESTS 1.1

A Package for Mrs. Jewls
Test Record Form

TEST RECORD FORM	Possible Score	Criterion Score	Student Score
Vocabulary: Target Vocabulary, Using Context	10	8	
Comprehension: Story Structure, Selection Test	10	8	
Decoding: VCV Syllable Pattern	10	8	
Language Arts: Complete Sentences	10	8	
TOTAL	40	32	

Total Student Score × 2.5 = _____ %

Test Record Form
© Houghton Mifflin Harcourt Publishing Company. All rights reserved.

Grade 5, Unit 1: School Spirit!

Name _____ Date _____

Lesson 1
WEEKLY TESTS 1.2

A Package for Mrs. Jewls
Vocabulary

Target Vocabulary, Using Context

*D*irections
Use what you know about the target vocabulary and using context to answer questions 1–10. For each question, circle the letter next to your answer choice.

1 What does the word "specialty" mean in the sentence below?

> The restaurant's specialty is making perfect pizza.

A chef
B hobby
C favorite food
D unique talent

2 What does the word "collapsed" mean in the sentence below?

> The house of cards collapsed just as I placed the last card on top.

A bent
B grew
C jumped
D fell

3 What does the word "disturbing" mean in the sentence below?

> Teddy kept disturbing us while we were doing our homework.

A helping
B bothering
C following
D entertaining

4 What does the word "interrupted" mean in the sentence below?

> The baby's crying interrupted our conversation.

A helped
B stopped
C changed
D reviewed

Go On

Vocabulary
© Houghton Mifflin Harcourt Publishing Company. All rights reserved.

Grade 5, Unit 1: School Spirit!

Lesson 1
WEEKLY TESTS 1.3

A Package for Mrs. Jewls
Vocabulary

Name _____ Date _____

5 What does the word "wobbled" mean in the sentence below?

> The toddler wobbled toward the door.

A ran quickly
B crawled slowly
C rolled unhappily
D walked unsteadily

6 What does the word "pursuit" mean in the sentence below?

> The athletes all tried their best in pursuit of the grand prize.

A a medal or trophy
B the end of a race
C something that holds money
D an effort to achieve

7 What does the word "vigorously" mean in the sentence below?

> I ran vigorously after my homework, but the wind carried it away before I could grab it.

A to move slowly
B in an uneasy way
C to give up
D in a strong way

8 What does the word "jubilant" mean in the sentence below?

> Allison felt jubilant when she heard the wonderful news.

A upset
B cold
C joyful
D impatient

9 What does the word "tendency" mean in the sentence below?

> That clock has a tendency to fall behind by a few minutes.

A soft
B rarity
C habit
D change

10 What does the word "urgent" mean in the sentence below?

> Oscar called his sister as soon as he got her urgent message.

A friendly
B automatic
C very important
D moving too much

STOP

Vocabulary

Grade 5, Unit 1: School Spirit!

Lesson 1
WEEKLY TESTS 1.4

Name _____ Date _____

A Package for Mrs. Jewls
Comprehension

Story Structure, Selection Test

Directions
Think back to the selection "A Package for Mrs. Jewls from Wayside School Is Falling Down" to answer questions 1–10. For each question, circle the letter next to your answer choice.

1 What is the **first** important event in the story?

  A Louis passes out balls during recess.
  B A truck horn honks and disturbs the students.
  C Louis starts cleaning up junk on the playground.
  D Students toss pieces of paper and pencils into the schoolyard.

2 Louis helps Mrs. Jewls receive her package by

  A calling Mrs. Jewls to come get the box
  B telling the delivery person that he is Mrs. Jewls
  C ordering the truck driver to stop honking the horn
  D taking the package to the school basement to keep it safe

3 Louis goes to Mrs. Jewls's classroom by

  A riding the elevator
  B climbing up the stairs
  C going down a long hallway
  D walking across the schoolyard

4 What causes Louis the **most** trouble in making sure that Mrs. Jewls gets her package?

  A Mrs. Mush is cooking mushrooms in the cafeteria.
  B The students cannot be interrupted while they are working.
  C The delivery person must give the package directly to Mrs. Jewls.
  D Mrs. Jewls's classroom is on the top floor of Wayside School.

Go On

Comprehension
© Houghton Mifflin Harcourt Publishing Company. All rights reserved.

Grade 5, Unit 1: School Spirit!

Name _____ Date _____

Lesson 1
WEEKLY TESTS 1.5

A Package for Mrs. Jewls
Comprehension

5 Louis knocks on the classroom door with his

  A shoe
  B head
  C hand
  D elbow

6 Louis is wrong when he believes that Wayside School students

  A do not like computers
  B like playing on a playground
  C are busy learning in their classrooms
  D hate to be interrupted when they are working

7 How does Mrs. Jewls solve the problem of letting Louis into the classroom?

  A She holds a spelling bee.
  B She opens the door for Louis herself.
  C She chooses her best student to open the door.
  D She flips a coin to decide who will open the door.

8 This story is told from the point of view of

  A Louis
  B Mrs. Jewls
  C the delivery person
  D a third-person narrator

9 Louis's actions are important because they show that the story is

  A sad
  B cruel
  C absurd
  D realistic

10 At the end of the story, Mrs. Jewls thanks Louis for

  A taking good care of her package
  B picking up the paper and pencils
  C putting the package where she wants it
  D helping her teach the students about gravity

Mark Student Reading Level:
____ Independent   ____ Instructional   ____ Listening

STOP

Comprehension
Grade 5, Unit 1: School Spirit!

Name _____ Date _____

Lesson 1
WEEKLY TESTS 1.6

VCV Syllable Pattern

A Package for Mrs. Jewls
Decoding

Directions
Use what you know about VCV syllable pattern to answer questions 1–10. Divide the underlined words into syllables. For each question, circle the letter next to your answer choice.

1 Sasha promised to take good care of our dog, Buck.

  A promi • sed
  B pro • mised
  C promis • ed
  D prom • ised

2 The teacher asked the students to be silent.

  A sil • ent
  B si • lent
  C sile • nt
  D s • ilent

3 The dog behaved well during the party.

  A beha • ved
  B behav • ed
  C beh • aved
  D be • haved

4 The ground was solid rock so it was hard to dig a hole.

  A sol • id
  B so • lid
  C soli • d
  D s • olid

5 The weather has been pleasant lately.

  A plea • sant
  B pleas • ant
  C ple • asant
  D pl • easant

6 Sheila will direct the movie.

  A dire • ct
  B dir • ect
  C di • rect
  D d • irect

Go On

Decoding
© Houghton Mifflin Harcourt Publishing Company. All rights reserved.

Grade 5, Unit 1: School Spirit!

Name _____ Date _____

Lesson 1
WEEKLY TESTS 1.7

A Package for Mrs. Jewls
Decoding

7 The large <u>shovel</u> is in the garage.

A sh • ovel
B shove • l
C sho • vel
D shov • el

8 Nellie read the <u>comics</u> yesterday.

A co • mics
B com • ics
C comi • cs
D c • omics

9 Opal was a very <u>rapid</u> skater.

A rap • id
B ra • pid
C rapi • d
D r • apid

10 Isaac was <u>aware</u> of the wind howling outside.

A awa • re
B awar • e
C a • ware
D aw • are

STOP

Decoding

© Houghton Mifflin Harcourt Publishing Company. All rights reserved.

Grade 5, Unit 1: School Spirit!

Name _____ Date _____

Lesson 1
WEEKLY TESTS 1.8

Complete Sentences

A Package for Mrs. Jewls
Language Arts

*D*irections
Use what you know about complete sentences to answer questions 1–10.
For each question, circle the letter next to your answer choice.

1 Which of the following is a complete sentence?

  A The icy wind.
  B The wind fast.
  C The wind felt icy.
  D The wind and rain.

2 Which of the following is a complete sentence?

  A Suzy and Jacob like.
  B Suzy likes reading books.
  C Suzy and Jacob might like.
  D Suzy reads and Jacob likes.

3 Which of the following is a complete sentence?

  A Because the story unbelievable.
  B Unbelievable stories are completely.
  C The story was completely unbelievable.
  D The story was almost unbelievable because.

4 Which of the following is a complete sentence?

  A The children lunch.
  B The playing children.
  C At noon, the playing children.
  D At noon, the children ate lunch.

5 Which of the following is a complete sentence?

  A And six more.
  B I want six more.
  C Five or six more.
  D Because of five more.

6 Which of the following is a complete sentence?

  A Bus stop at.
  B The bus stop.
  C The bus stopped.
  D Because bus stopped.

Go On

Language Arts
© Houghton Mifflin Harcourt Publishing Company. All rights reserved.

Grade 5, Unit 1: School Spirit!

Name _____ Date _____

Lesson 1
WEEKLY TESTS 1.9

A Package for Mrs. Jewls
Language Arts

7 Which of the following is a complete sentence?

A Do man go and?
B Do you know if?
C Who is man and?
D Who is that man?

8 Which of the following is a complete sentence?

A Bee stung the mark on Syd.
B The mark on Syd's arm was.
C Because the stinger in Syd's arm.
D The bee stung Syd and left a mark.

9 Which of the following is a complete sentence?

A I read so that.
B Reading can be.
C I like many books.
D As fiction and nonfiction.

10 Which of the following is a complete sentence?

A The best the amusement park.
B The amusement park is the because.
C We will go to the amusement park.
D Because the amusement park is the.

STOP

Language Arts
© Houghton Mifflin Harcourt Publishing Company. All rights reserved.

Grade 5, Unit 1: School Spirit!

Name _____ Date _____

Lesson 2
WEEKLY TESTS 2.1

Ultimate Field Trip 5: Blasting Off to Space Academy
Test Record Form

TEST RECORD FORM	Possible Score	Criterion Score	Student Score
Vocabulary: Target Vocabulary, Prefixes *non-*, *un-*, *dis-*, *mis-*	10	8	
Comprehension: Text and Graphic Features, Selection Test	10	8	
Decoding: Vowel Sounds in VCV Syllable Patterns	10	8	
Language Arts: Kinds of Sentences	10	8	
TOTAL	40	32	
		Total Student Score × 2.5 =	%

Go On

Test Record Form
© Houghton Mifflin Harcourt Publishing Company. All rights reserved.

Grade 5, Unit 1: School Spirit!

Name _____   Date _____

Lesson 2
WEEKLY TESTS 2.2

Ultimate Field Trip 5:
Blasting Off
to Space Academy
Vocabulary

Target Vocabulary, Prefixes *non-*, *un-*, *dis-*, *mis-*

*D*irections
Use what you know about the target vocabulary and prefixes to answer questions 1–10. For each question, circle the letter next to your answer choice.

1 What does the word "simulate" mean in the sentence below?

   The students wanted to simulate what it was like to live as a pioneer.

   A draw
   B imitate
   C research
   D appreciate

2 What does the word "delicate" mean in the sentence below?

   The scientist studied the delicate flower.

   A simply designed
   B brightly colored
   C rarely grown
   D easily damaged

3 What does the word "adjusted" mean in the sentence below?

   Toby adjusted the brakes on his bicycle.

   A broke
   B changed
   C replaced
   D purchased

4 What does the word "tethered" mean in the sentence below?

   The rancher tethered his horse to a tree.

   A tied
   B rode
   C walked
   D balanced

5 What does the word "acute" mean in the sentence below?

   The cat has an acute sense of hearing.

   A fair
   B crazy
   C brave
   D sharp

Vocabulary
© Houghton Mifflin Harcourt Publishing Company. All rights reserved.

Grade 5, Unit 1: School Spirit!

Lesson 2
WEEKLY TESTS 2.3

Name _____ Date _____

Ultimate Field Trip 5: Blasting Off to Space Academy
Vocabulary

6 What does the word "nonsense" mean in the sentence below?

> Dad wondered what nonsense the children were up to since it was too quiet in the house.

A sweet dreams
B foolish actions
C library research
D household chores

7 What does the word "uneasy" mean in the sentence below?

> The horse seemed uneasy as the storm approached.

A lazy
B angry
C jealous
D disturbed

8 What does the word "disorder" mean in the sentence below?

> When my mother saw how much disorder was in my room, she ordered me to clean it right away.

A put in order
B lack of order
C too much order
D in the wrong order

9 What does the word "misunderstand" mean in the sentence below?

> Barbara feared she would misunderstand the directions and get lost.

A give away
B never read
C not figure out
D put in the wrong place

10 What does the word "unnoticed" mean in the sentence below?

> Many people walked by the nest, but the baby squirrels were unnoticed.

A not seen
B not moving
C not playing
D not sleeping

STOP

Vocabulary
© Houghton Mifflin Harcourt Publishing Company. All rights reserved.

Grade 5, Unit 1: School Spirit!

Name _____ Date _____

Text and Graphic Features, Selection Test

Lesson 2
WEEKLY TESTS 2.4

**Ultimate Field Trip 5:
Blasting Off
to Space Academy**
Comprehension

Directions

Think back to the selection "Ultimate Field Trip 5: Blasting Off to Space Academy" to answer questions 1–10. For each question, circle the letter next to your answer choice.

1 Which quote from the selection **best** expresses the topic?

  A What's the best part of being an astronaut?
  B The last time astronauts walked on the moon was 1972...
  C ...some kids take the first step by going to the U.S. Space Academy...
  D It takes a lot of practice to learn how to function in such a different environment.

2 The photograph on page 51 shows what it feels like to

  A do a bunny hop
  B walk on the moon
  C jump on a trampoline
  D practice the high jump

3 The "Amazing Space Facts" text boxes tell you details about

  A real space exploration
  B how to become an astronaut
  C the kids' visit to Space Academy
  D how astronauts move in low and no gravity

4 To quickly find information about the 5DF Chair, you would

  A read the entire selection
  B look at the photographs
  C read the "Amazing Space Facts" text boxes
  D scan the selection for a heading about the chair

5 To find information about NASA's Space Shot, you could look at all these features except a

  A text box
  B caption
  C heading
  D photograph

6 The **best** place in the selection to find information about America's first space station is in a

  A sidebar
  B text box
  C photograph
  D caption

Comprehension
© Houghton Mifflin Harcourt Publishing Company. All rights reserved.

Grade 5, Unit 1: School Spirit!

Name _____ Date _____

Lesson 2
WEEKLY TESTS 2.5

Ultimate Field Trip 5: Blasting Off to Space Academy
Comprehension

7 What is the purpose of the text box on page 57?

   A It describes the topic in a heading.
   B It presents some facts about the Hubble Space Telescope.
   C It shows a photograph of kids working together underwater.
   D It tells the steps the kids take to quickly build a cube together.

8 The section of the selection with the heading "The Pool" tells how astronauts

   A build cubes underwater
   B learn how to hold their breath
   C pretend they are working in weightlessness
   D use a swimming pool to hold a model of the space shuttle

9 Under which heading can you learn ways you can work in the space program?

   A Blast Off!
   B Space Shot
   C On the Training Floor
   D The Multi-Axis Trainer (MAT)

10 You can only learn the story of the children visiting the Space Academy by reading the

   A text boxes
   B whole selection
   C selection and text boxes
   D introduction to the selection

Mark Student Reading Level:
____ Independent   ____ Instructional   ____ Listening

STOP

Comprehension
© Houghton Mifflin Harcourt Publishing Company. All rights reserved.

Grade 5, Unit 1: School Spirit!

Name _____ **Date** _____

Lesson 2
WEEKLY TESTS 2.6

Vowel Sounds in VCV Syllable Patterns

Ultimate Field Trip 5: Blasting Off to Space Academy
Decoding

*D*irections
Use what you know about vowel sounds in VCV syllable patterns to answer the questions. For each question, circle the letter next to your answer choice.

1 Which word has the same vowel sound as the a in "agent"?

 A ray
 B ham
 C gravel
 D disaster

2 Which word has the same vowel sound as the o in "column"?

 A bowl
 B cough
 C hospital
 D antelope

3 Which word has the same vowel sound as the i in "ivory"?

 A basin
 B fright
 C discuss
 D century

4 Which word has the same vowel sound as the o in "poverty"?

 A bloom
 B growth
 C oxygen
 D astound

5 Which word has the same vowel sound as the a in "eraser"?

 A art
 B goal
 C raid
 D call

6 Which word has the same vowel sound as the a in "labor"?

 A actual
 B frantic
 C capsule
 D neighbor

Decoding
© Houghton Mifflin Harcourt Publishing Company. All rights reserved.

Grade 5, Unit 1: School Spirit!

Name _____ Date _____

Lesson 2
WEEKLY TESTS 2.7

Ultimate Field Trip 5: Blasting Off to Space Academy
Decoding

7 Which word has the same vowel sound as the i in "olive"?

A silk
B deny
C plain
D white

8 Which word has the same vowel sound as the i in "miner"?

A sky
B tray
C field
D bitter

9 Which word has the same vowel sound as the u in "refuge"?

A tub
B few
C shook
D league

10 Which word has the same vowel sound as the a in "taxi"?

A sale
B paid
C apple
D crawl

STOP

Decoding
© Houghton Mifflin Harcourt Publishing Company. All rights reserved.

Grade 5, Unit 1: School Spirit!

Name _____ Date _____

Lesson 2
WEEKLY TESTS 2.8

Kinds of Sentences

Ultimate Field Trip 5:
Blasting Off
to Space Academy
Language Arts

Directions
Use what you know about kinds of sentences to answer questions 1–10. For each question, circle the letter next to your answer choice.

1 Which of these is an EXCLAMATORY sentence?

A That tree just blew over!
B My sister drove to the city.
C Our aunt lives in North Carolina.
D Have you ever been in a bad storm?

2 Which of these is an INTERROGATIVE sentence?

A I used to know a girl named Betsy.
B Scientists study how ants work together.
C Do you know why hurricanes have names?
D Grandma and Grandpa are finally coming to visit!

3 Which of these is an IMPERATIVE sentence?

A The volcano is erupting!
B Please go patch the roof.
C Debbie has to clean up her room.
D What time is the movie on Saturday?

4 Which of these is an INTERROGATIVE sentence?

A The picnic will be at the park.
B Did you read that book last night?
C Find the newspaper and bring it back.
D It rained over two inches in one hour!

5 Which of these is an IMPERATIVE sentence?

A What an incredible day it was!
B Did you see that butterfly land?
C Watch the news on television tonight.
D We drove to New Orleans, Louisiana.

6 Which of these is an EXCLAMATORY sentence?

A Please pass the juice.
B Where does this bus stop?
C I bought a new shirt for school.
D Watch out for that ant hill!

Language Arts

Grade 5, Unit 1: School Spirit!

Lesson 2
WEEKLY TESTS 2.9

Ultimate Field Trip 5: Blasting Off to Space Academy
Language Arts

Name _____ Date _____

7 Which of these is a DECLARATIVE sentence?

   A Tom played basketball.
   B Where is the art teacher?
   C Stop beating those drums!
   D Patty's dog won first prize!

8 Which of these is an INTERROGATIVE sentence?

   A Dad cannot find his car keys.
   B Where did Joel put the flashlight?
   C This is my first trip on an airplane!
   D Take out the trash before you go to school.

9 Which of these is a DECLARATIVE sentence?

   A The batter hit a home run!
   B Can you please wait by the gate?
   C That window was already broken.
   D Is it time for the children to go to bed?

10 Which of these is a DECLARATIVE sentence?

   A Look at that wild horse!
   B Who came to Luanne's party?
   C Have you seen Joe play football?
   D Some birds fly south for the winter.

STOP

Language Arts
© Houghton Mifflin Harcourt Publishing Company. All rights reserved.

Grade 5, Unit 1: School Spirit!

Name _____ Date _____

Lesson 3
WEEKLY TESTS 3.1

Off and Running
Test Record Form

TEST RECORD FORM	Possible Score	Criterion Score	Student Score
Skills in Context: Compare and Contrast, Target Vocabulary	10	8	
Vocabulary: Target Vocabulary, Multiple-Meaning Words	10	8	
Comprehension: Compare and Contrast, Selection Test	10	8	
Decoding: VCCV Pattern	10	8	
Language Arts: Compound Sentences	10	8	
TOTAL	50	40	
		Total Student Score × 2 =	%

Test Record Form
© Houghton Mifflin Harcourt Publishing Company. All rights reserved.

Grade 5, Unit 1: School Spirit!

Name _____ Date _____

Compare and Contrast, Target Vocabulary

Lesson 3
WEEKLY TESTS 3.2

Off and Running
Skills in Context

***D**irections*
Read the selection. Then read each question that follows the selection. Decide which is the best answer to each question. For each question, circle the letter next to your answer choice.

Running for School Council

Tameka fumbled with a set of papers as she got ready for school. Mom prodded her to move faster. Then she saw a worried look on her daughter's face. "What is wrong, honey?" Mom asked.

The fifth grader stared at the ground. She hesitated to tell her mom. Finally, she said, "I am going to run for school council. I filled out the application last night, and I am ready to turn it in today. The problem is that I have not told Mary that I am doing this. She is my best friend. I am afraid she will be upset that I will not have as much time to spend with her."

Mom wondered what words of wisdom she could share with her daughter. Then she said, "You and Mary have been friends for a long time. I think you will be able to keep your friendship, even if you cannot spend as much time together."

Tameka knew what words were coming next. She smiled as she said them with her mother, "Change is a natural part of growing up." Tameka kissed her mother on the cheek and rushed out the door to catch the school bus.

When the bus arrived at school, Tameka hurried to the office to turn in her form for school council. Two forms dropped into the box at exactly the same time. Tameka looked up to see Mary standing next to her. Mary smiled her usual grin and greeted Tameka. The girls broke out giggling. They realized that they had both kept a secret from their best friend. They talked about how they were worried about hurting each other's feelings. This made them realize just how strong their friendship was.

Mary and Tameka were running for different offices on the school council. They decided that they would help each other prepare for the election. The girls made arrangements to meet on Saturday to start planning their strategy.

When the weekend arrived, the girls met after breakfast at Mary's house. Tameka carefully unrolled the two pieces of poster board she brought with her. Mary pulled out a box of colored markers. Both girls made a poster to tell why they would make good candidates for the council.

Go On

Then they decorated their posters with pictures to show some of the things they would do if elected. When they were done, they admired each other's work.

On Monday, the girls hung their posters on the wall in the main hall. They were surprised by the number of students running for the council. The walls were lined with posters by students who had good ideas. The girls knew that it would be hard to win the election. However, they were determined to serve on the council together.

The next step would be to get ready for the debate. It was going to be held next month. The girls had a lot to learn. They needed to know how to have this type of discussion. They also needed to learn about topics that the council would address. This would help them decide if they were for or against each issue.

The girls studied. They practiced talking about their viewpoints. The days passed into weeks. Finally, the big day was here. The girls sat on the stage. They smiled at each other. They waited for their turn to share their point of view. At the end of the day, many students told Tameka and Mary they had done a good job. The election was right around the corner. The girls were looking forward to hearing the results. They knew that no matter what the outcome was, they would still be best friends.

Name _____ Date _____

Lesson 3
WEEKLY TESTS 3.4

Off and Running
Skills in Context

1 What does the word "hesitated" mean as used in the passage?

A to talk quickly
B to pause in fear
C to show courage
D to reveal the truth

2 What problem does Tameka have at the beginning of the story?

A She does not want to go to school.
B She forgot to complete her homework.
C She is afraid her best friend will be mad at her.
D She has not filled out her application for school council.

3 What words has Tameka's mom said before?

A "What is wrong, honey?"
B "Change is a natural part of growing up."
C "You and Mary have been friends a long time."
D "I think you will be able to keep your friendship, even if you cannot spend as much time together."

4 What do Tameka and Mary both do?

A They ride the same bus.
B They ask their mom for help.
C They apply to run for school council.
D They play on the same basketball team.

5 What happens when the girls realize they have kept a secret from each other?

A They get angry and start to argue.
B They throw away their applications.
C They realize they have a strong friendship.
D They choose to run for different offices on the council.

6 What do all the candidates that are running for the council have to do?

A make a poster
B write a speech
C stay after school
D work with a partner

Go On

Skills in Context
© Houghton Mifflin Harcourt Publishing Company. All rights reserved.

Grade 5, Unit 1: School Spirit!

Name _____ Date _____

Lesson 3
WEEKLY TESTS 3.5

Off and Running
Skills in Context

7 What problem did the girls solve by working together?

A They got to serve on the council.
B They got to see who was the best artist.
C They got to spend time with each other.
D They got to learn how to fill out an application.

8 What happened **after** the debate?

A The candidates drew posters.
B The students elected council members.
C The candidates turned in an application.
D The students went home for the summer.

9 What does the word "debate" mean as it is used in the passage?

A a strategy used to reach a goal
B a friendship that lasts a long time
C a discussion to share different viewpoints
D a place for students to have a council meeting

10 Which question is not answered in the story?

A What was the purpose of the debate?
B Who was elected to the school council?
C Where did the students hang their posters?
D Why did Tameka and Mary start to giggle in the office?

STOP

Skills in Context

Grade 5, Unit 1: School Spirit!

Name _____ Date _____

Lesson 3
WEEKLY TESTS 3.6

Off and Running
Vocabulary

Target Vocabulary, Multiple-Meaning Words

Directions
Use what you know about the target vocabulary and multiple-meaning words to answer questions 1–10. For each question, circle the letter next to your answer choice.

1 What does the word "scanned" mean in the sentence below?

> I scanned the crowd to see if I could find my friends.

A shouted at
B examined closely
C guessed the size of
D asked questions about

2 What does the word "prodded" mean in the sentence below?

> The teacher prodded her students to do a science fair project.

A asked
B pushed
C wished
D guessed

3 What does the word "beckoned" mean in the sentence below?

> Zaniya beckoned to her brother to peek at the baby birds in the nest.

A sang
B looked
C laughed
D signaled

4 What does the word "inflated" mean in the sentence below?

> The girl inflated the tire before attempting to ride her bicycle.

A filled with air
B fixed with a patch
C placed water inside
D cleaned with soap

Go On

Vocabulary
© Houghton Mifflin Harcourt Publishing Company. All rights reserved.

Grade 5, Unit 1: School Spirit!

Lesson 3
WEEKLY TESTS 3.7

Name _____ Date _____

Off and Running
Vocabulary

5 What does the word "gradually" mean in the sentence below?

Isabel gradually figured out how to solve her problem.

A usually
B quickly
C little by little
D with great effort

6 What does the word "appeal" mean in the sentence below?

The criminal made an appeal to the judge.

A a sincere request
B to like something
C attraction
D to charge with a crime

7 What does the word "connected" mean in the sentence below?

The garage is connected to the house.

A joined
B transferred
C hit successfully
D had a special bond

8 What does the word "stub" mean in the sentence below?

Be careful that you do not stub your toe in the dark.

A A tree stump
B Part of a ticket
C To pull up by the roots
D To strike against an object

9 What does the word "operate" mean in the sentence below?

The doctor will need to operate to remove the girl's tonsils.

A to do a certain job
B to perform surgery
C to have a military action
D to cause something to work

10 What does the word "recess" mean in the sentence below?

The children played basketball during recess.

A to stop a trial
B to take a break
C a secret or hidden place
D a time for rest and relaxing

STOP

Vocabulary
© Houghton Mifflin Harcourt Publishing Company. All rights reserved.

Grade 5, Unit 1: School Spirit!

Compare and Contrast, Selection Test

Off and Running
Comprehension

Directions
Think back to the selection "Off and Running" to answer questions 1–10. For each question, circle the letter next to your answer choice.

1 Miata shows she is more serious about school than Rudy by

A following the rules
B running for class president
C chewing gum with her mouth closed
D promising to pay students to work around the school

2 How is Rudy different from Miata?

A He seems more realistic.
B He seems more popular.
C He seems less energetic.
D He seems less confident.

3 Miata's campaign promises differ from Rudy's because they focus on

A helping teachers
B changing school rules
C cleaning up the school
D making students happy

4 How is Miata different during the debate compared to when she practiced her speech at home?

A She is happier talking to a crowd.
B She acts more confident at school.
C She likes to interact with the audience.
D She loses faith in her ability to persuade students.

5 If Miata wins the election and keeps her campaign promises, the school will become

A less fun
B more fun
C less beautiful
D more beautiful

Go On

Comprehension

Grade 5, Unit 1: School Spirit!

Name _____ Date _____

Lesson 3
WEEKLY TESTS 3.9

Off and Running
Comprehension

6 When Rudy compares himself to Miata as president, he says

A he would be a great president, and she would be a good president
B he would be a fun president, and she would be a serious president
C she would be a good president, and he would be a smart president
D she would be a gloomy president, and he would be a popular president

7 The students in the audience

A clap harder for Rudy
B laugh at Rudy's ideas
C chant for Miata's ideas
D applaud harder for Miata

8 Miata's father helps her see the difference between

A her and Rudy
B fun and seriousness
C popularity and service
D behaving well and misbehaving

9 What do both Rudy and Miata believe?

A Miata has good ideas.
B Girls like Rudy better.
C Boys will vote for Miata.
D Rudy can fulfill his promises.

10 Miata's campaign promises appeal more to

A girls
B boys
C all the parents
D all the students

Mark Student Reading Level:
____ Independent   ____ Instructional   ____ Listening

STOP

Comprehension

Grade 5, Unit 1: School Spirit!

VCCV Pattern

Lesson 3
WEEKLY TESTS 3.10

Off and Running
Decoding

Directions Use what you know about VCCV pattern to answer questions 1–10. Divide the underlined words into syllables. For each question, circle the letter next to your answer choice.

1 The snow was like a fine powder.

A powde • r
B po • wder
C pow • der
D powd • er

2 It is rude to whisper secrets in public.

A whi • sper
B whis • per
C whisp • er
D wh • is • per

3 The panda's hunger was satisfied by the bamboo tree.

A hu • nger
B hun • ger
C hung • er
D h • unger

4 The public is entitled to know the truth.

A pu • blic
B pub • lic
C publ • ic
D publi • c

5 Do not excite the baby before bedtime.

A exci • te
B exc • ite
C ex • cite
D e • xcite

6 The young pianist will compose a song.

A co • mpose
B comp • ose
C c • ompose
D com • pose

Go On

Decoding
© Houghton Mifflin Harcourt Publishing Company. All rights reserved.

Grade 5, Unit 1: School Spirit!

Lesson 3
WEEKLY TESTS 3.11

Name _____ Date _____

Off and Running
Decoding

7 Perhaps they decided not to join us.

A pe • rhaps
B perha • ps
C perh • aps
D per • haps

8 My dog hid under the couch when he heard the thunder.

A thun • der
B thu • nder
C thund • er
D th • under

9 The procedure will not be painful.

A pai • nful
B pa • inful
C pain • ful
D painf • ul

10 Any person can join the team.

A pe • rson
B perso • n
C per • son
D pers • on

STOP

Decoding
© Houghton Mifflin Harcourt Publishing Company. All rights reserved.

Grade 5, Unit 1: School Spirit!

Lesson 3
WEEKLY TESTS 3.12

Name _____ Date _____

Compound Sentences

Off and Running
Language Arts

Directions
Use what you know about compound sentences to answer questions 1–10. For each question, circle the letter next to your answer choice.

1 What is the complete subject of this sentence?

Lisa's best friend Sue is a really nice person.

A is a really
B best friend
C a really nice person
D Lisa's best friend Sue

2 What is the complete subject of this sentence?

Harvey, the delivery man, was very strong.

A was
B was very strong
C the delivery man
D Harvey, the delivery man

3 What is the complete predicate of this sentence?

Alexandra, the littlest puppy in the litter, will be mine.

A Alexandra
B will be mine
C the littlest puppy in the litter
D Alexandra, the littlest puppy

4 What is the complete predicate of this sentence?

The calm ocean was perfect for swimming.

A was
B ocean
C calm ocean was perfect
D was perfect for swimming

Go On

Language Arts

Grade 5, Unit 1: School Spirit!

Lesson 3
WEEKLY TESTS 3.13

Name _____ Date _____

Off and Running
Language Arts

5 Which of these is a compound sentence?

  A Officer Juarez had a kind, friendly smile.
  B In October, the leaves begin to change colors.
  C Ami went to the store, but she forgot to buy milk.
  D Before the train departed, the passengers boarded.

6 Which of these is a compound sentence?

  A After the show, the children clapped loudly.
  B The doctor, who was new in town, bought a house.
  C Mr. Thomas painted his fence red, white, and blue.
  D Tom fed the chickens, and Julie collected the eggs.

7 Which of these is a compound sentence?

  A Jordan needed some nails, so she went to the hardware store.
  B Long ago, huge creatures called dinosaurs roamed the planet.
  C Steven played basketball with Dani, Carson, Gail, and Robert.
  D When Beth moved to Austin, Texas, she was eleven years old.

8 Which sentence is written correctly?

  A Domingo finished all of his homework, he still had to study for his test.
  B Domingo finished all of his homework, but he still had to study for his test.
  C Domingo finished all, of his homework, but he still had to study for his test.
  D Domingo finished all of his homework but he still had to study for his test.

Language Arts
© Houghton Mifflin Harcourt Publishing Company. All rights reserved.

Grade 5, Unit 1: School Spirit!

Name _____ Date _____

9 Which sentence is written correctly?

A Gina got a new kitten she invited her friends over to see it.
B Gina got a new kitten, she invited her friends over to see it.
C Gina got a new kitten, and she invited her friends over to see it.
D Gina got a new kitten but she invited her friends over to see it.

10 Which sentence is written correctly?

A Lisa will lend Sue the book, she will give it to her as a present.
B Lisa will lend Sue the book, or she will give it to her as a present.
C Lisa will lend Sue the book she will give it to her as a present.
D Lisa will lend Sue the book but she will give it to her as a present.

STOP

Name _____ Date _____

Lesson 4
WEEKLY TESTS 4.1

**Double Dutch:
A Celebration of Jump
Rope, Rhyme,
and Sisterhood**

Test Record Form

TEST RECORD FORM	Possible Score	Criterion Score	Student Score
Vocabulary: Target Vocabulary, Suffixes *-ion, -tion*	10	8	
Comprehension: Sequence of Events, Selection Test	10	8	
Decoding: Digraphs in Multisyllable Words	10	8	
Language Arts: Common and Proper Nouns	10	8	
TOTAL	40	32	

Total Student Score × 2.5 = _____ %

Test Record Form
© Houghton Mifflin Harcourt Publishing Company. All rights reserved.

Grade 5, Unit 1: School Spirit!

Name _____ Date _____

Lesson 4
WEEKLY TESTS 4.2

Target Vocabulary, Suffixes -ion, -tion

**Double Dutch:
A Celebration of
Jump Rope, Rhyme,
and Sisterhood**
Vocabulary

Directions
Use what you know about the target vocabulary and suffixes to answer questions 1–10. For each question, circle the letter next to your answer choice.

1 What does the word "competition" mean in the sentence below?

The skaters had a competition to see who could skate fastest.

A timer
B lesson
C contest
D statement

2 What does the word "identical" mean in the sentence below?

The two shells looked identical.

A similar
B uniform
C exactly alike
D completely different

3 What does the word "element" mean in the sentence below?

The fan was the element that failed to work.

A part
B strap
C quarter
D mixture

4 What does the word "routine" mean in the sentence below?

Brushing your teeth is an important part of your morning routine.

A a walk in the park
B a household chore
C a regular course of action
D a way to learn new things

Go On

Vocabulary
© Houghton Mifflin Harcourt Publishing Company. All rights reserved.

Grade 5, Unit 1: School Spirit!

Name _____ Date _____

**Lesson 4
WEEKLY TESTS 4.3**

**Double Dutch:
A Celebration of
Jump Rope, Rhyme,
and Sisterhood**
Vocabulary

5 What does the word "unison" mean in the sentence below?

The girls started to giggle in unison.

A at the same time
B before going outside
C with a crowd of people
D while making silly faces

6 What does the word "appreciation" mean in the sentence below?

The mayor gave the students a certificate in appreciation for all their hard work.

A favor
B school
C thanks
D evidence

7 What does the word "pronunciation" mean in the sentence below?

The teacher had his students practice the pronunciation of the vocabulary words.

A how to say something
B how to read something
C how to spell something
D how to write something

8 What does the word "decision" mean in the sentence below?

Gregor made the best decision he could based on the facts that he had.

A choice
B report
C apology
D disguise

9 What does the word "explosion" mean in the sentence below?

The loud clap of thunder sounded like an explosion.

A the beating of a drum
B something blowing up
C the applause of a crowd
D something winding down

10 What does the word "population" mean in the sentence below?

Because there is plenty of food, the rabbit population is growing very quickly.

A geography
B emergency
C green plants
D total number

STOP

Vocabulary

Grade 5, Unit 1: School Spirit!

Name _____ Date _____

Sequence of Events, Selection Test

Lesson 4
WEEKLY TESTS 4.4

Double Dutch: A Celebration of Jump Rope, Rhyme, and Sisterhood
Comprehension

*D*irections
Think back to the selection "Double Dutch: A Celebration of Jump Rope, Rhyme, and Sisterhood" to answer questions 1–10. For each question, circle the letter next to your answer choice.

1 At the beginning of the selection, five girls are

  A an award-winning Double Dutch team
  B hoping to become a Double Dutch team
  C learning to jump rope and practicing Double Dutch
  D sad after losing their first Double Dutch competition

2 Which sentence indicates that the selection is moving back in history?

  A *Coach Rockett was thrilled but intimidated.*
  B *In the ropes, it seems that the Steppers defy gravity.*
  C *Life for the Snazzy Steppers wasn't always so sweet.*
  D *Coach Rockett even wrote a song to help teach his girls how to jump…*

3 The **first** thing Coach Rockett does is

  A learn to jump rope himself
  B organize a Double Dutch team
  C get an idea by looking out the window
  D buy several hundred yards of clothesline

4 Between the team's first competition in Harlem and their win in New York, the girls

  A are angry
  B quit the team
  C stop practicing their styles
  D do better at each competition

5 Which do the girls do **last** when starting to jump Double Dutch?

  A start to sing songs
  B practice their moves
  C begin turning ropes
  D jump to a new rhyme

Go On

Comprehension
© Houghton Mifflin Harcourt Publishing Company. All rights reserved.

Grade 5, Unit 1: School Spirit!

Name _____ Date _____

Lesson 4
WEEKLY TESTS 4.5

**Double Dutch:
A Celebration of
Jump Rope, Rhyme,
and Sisterhood**
Comprehension

6 Which shows the correct sequence of steps Coach Rockett took to form his team?

   A He studied the Internet; he had an idea; he made a flyer.
   B He visited other schools; he studied books; he wrote a song.
   C He made a flyer; he learned how to jump himself; he bought clothesline.
   D He bought clothesline; he learned how to jump himself; he made a flyer.

7 In the rhyme about Tiny Tim, what happens **right after** the puppy drinks the water?

   A The doctor jumps in.
   B The nurse jumps out.
   C The puppy swallows a bar of soap.
   D The singer puts the puppy in the bathtub.

8 When asked about their favorite part of competition, which girl answers **last**?

   A Erika
   B Peggy
   C Debbie
   D Katelyn

9 The Snazzy Steppers become best friends

   A before they join the team
   B when Coach Rockett tells them to
   C the first time they win a first-place trophy
   D after they compete together for a long time

10 Of all the girls, Lanieequah learned Double Dutch

   A first
   B second
   C fourth
   D fifth

Mark Student Reading Level:
___ Independent   ___ Instructional   ___ Listening

STOP

Comprehension
© Houghton Mifflin Harcourt Publishing Company. All rights reserved.

Grade 5, Unit 1: School Spirit!

Name _____ Date _____

Lesson 4
WEEKLY TESTS 4.6

Digraphs in Multisyllable Words

**Double Dutch:
A Celebration of
Jump Rope, Rhyme,
and Sisterhood**
Decoding

Directions
Use what you know about digraphs in multisyllable words to complete the sentences. For each question, circle the letter next to your answer choice.

1 Yesterday I went to the mall to make a

  A purthase
  B purshase
  C purchase
  D purcase

2 When the trick did not work, the magician felt

  A foolith
  B foolish
  C foolich
  D foolitch

3 The man in the painting looked

  A youthful
  B youshful
  C youchful
  D youtchful

4 Mary decided to give away some old

  A clothes
  B cloches
  C closhes
  D clotches

5 The farmer planted fields of

  A theat
  B cheat
  C sheet
  D wheat

6 When Grandma sewed quilts, she always used a

  A thimble
  B chimble
  C shimble
  D whimble

Go On

Decoding

Grade 5, Unit 1: School Spirit!

Name _____ Date _____

Lesson 4
WEEKLY TESTS 4.7

**Double Dutch:
A Celebration of
Jump Rope, Rhyme,
and Sisterhood**
Decoding

7 Jason could not hear over the clatter of the

    A mathines
    B machines
    C mashines
    D matchines

8 One animal that is extinct is the

    A mammosh
    B mammoch
    C mammoth
    D mammotch

9 The workers dug a very deep

    A dith
    B dish
    C dich
    D ditch

10 The children sat down to play a game of

    A theckers
    B sheckers
    C checkers
    D wheckers

STOP

Lesson 4
WEEKLY TESTS 4.8

Name _____ Date _____

Common and Proper Nouns

**Double Dutch:
A Celebration of
Jump Rope, Rhyme,
and Sisterhood**
Language Arts

*D*irections
Use what you know about common and proper nouns to answer questions 1–10. For each question, circle the letter next to your answer choice.

1 Which sentence is written correctly?

  A There is a Mission in san Antonio.
  B My Aunt lives in roanoke, Virginia.
  C We went swimming in the gulf of Mexico.
  D Megan took a trip to Texas and New Mexico.

2 Which sentence is written correctly?

  A The Sangre de cristo mountains are beautiful.
  B We watched the clouds drift over sandia peak.
  C Uncle George saw bats fly out of Carlsbad Caverns.
  D I think suki would like the balloon Festival in albuquerque.

3 Which sentence is written correctly?

  A The white house is in washington, D.C.
  B Lenny was watching the Wildlife at cades cove.
  C The Smoky Mountains are located in North Carolina.
  D Uncle martin moved from England to the united states.

4 Which sentence is written correctly?

  A Mr. Hernandez quickly boarded the Jet.
  B The water was as cold as ice at Eagle Falls.
  C The Family went hiking through newfound Gap.
  D The Students attended graham elementary school.

Go On

Language Arts
© Houghton Mifflin Harcourt Publishing Company. All rights reserved.

Grade 5, Unit 1: School Spirit!

Lesson 4
WEEKLY TESTS 4.9

Double Dutch: A Celebration of Jump Rope, Rhyme, and Sisterhood
Language Arts

5. Which sentence is written correctly?

   A Has Dr. anderson ever traveled to Japan?
   B The Smiths saw the Ruins in Rome, Italy.
   C David plans to go to the market on Wednesday.
   D Our Neighborhood will celebrate New Year's Eve.

6. Which sentence is written correctly?

   A We get the Newspaper every Thursday.
   B The girl worked in a Theater in London.
   C To get to our house, turn left on Strawberry Lane.
   D The students went to the Museum for their field trip.

7. Which sentence is written correctly?

   A It started to snow in December.
   B Hansel knows how to speak german.
   C The Fog floated up from the Pecos River.
   D The children picked up the Garbage from the lawn.

8. Which sentence is written correctly?

   A What Time does the Movie begin?
   B Hillary waited for Mother by the mailbox.
   C Do you know if sarah is waiting at the Bus Stop?
   D Franklin is a large Cat with black and white Fur.

9. Which sentence is written correctly?

   A There are many fish in Lime Creek.
   B My aunt Sue and uncle Jim live next door.
   C Dana is the best player on the Soccer Team.
   D The National Archives has many important Documents.

10. Which sentence is written correctly?

    A Dad works on the old Car in the Garage.
    B People lived long after the time of Dinosaurs.
    C Paul Revere was a famous American colonist.
    D Tourists enjoy visiting the great wall in China.

STOP

Language Arts

Grade 5, Unit 1: School Spirit!

Name _____ Date _____

Lesson 5
WEEKLY TESTS 5.1

Elisa's Diary
Test Record Form

TEST RECORD FORM	Possible Score	Criterion Score	Student Score
Vocabulary: Target Vocabulary, Suffixes -ly, -ful	10	8	
Comprehension: Theme, Selection Test	10	8	
Decoding: Stressed and Unstressed Syllables	10	8	
Language Arts: Singular and Plural Nouns	10	8	
TOTAL	40	32	
		Total Student Score × 2.5 =	%

Test Record Form
© Houghton Mifflin Harcourt Publishing Company. All rights reserved.

Grade 5, Unit 1: School Spirit!

Name _____   Date _____

Lesson 5
WEEKLY TESTS 5.2

Target Vocabulary, Suffixes *-ly, -ful*

Elisa's Diary
Vocabulary

*D*irections
Use what you know about the target vocabulary and suffixes to answer questions 1–10. For each question, circle the letter next to your answer choice.

1 What does the word "opponents" mean in the sentence below?

> The Eagles wondered how hard it would be to beat their opponents.

A rivals
B bosses
C servants
D messengers

2 What does the word "embarrassed" mean in the sentence below?

> The clown acted embarrassed when his hair turned blue.

A brilliant
B crushed
C ashamed
D reasonable

3 What does the word "typically" mean in the sentence below?

> These butterflies typically live in warmer climates.

A usually
B scarcely
C desperately
D independently

4 What does the word "brutal" mean in the sentence below?

> Polar bears are used to brutal weather conditions.

A crisp
B harsh
C rainy
D warm

Vocabulary
Grade 5, Unit 1: School Spirit!

Name _____   Date _____

Lesson 5
WEEKLY TESTS 5.3

Elisa's Diary
Vocabulary

5 What does the word "obvious" mean in the sentence below?

> Nathan knew there had to be an obvious answer to the mystery.

A deeply buried
B amazingly clever
C easily discovered
D surprisingly famous

6 What does the word "obediently" mean in the sentence below?

> The dog obediently followed his owner.

A jumping up
B taking time
C being faithful
D looking ahead

7 What does the word "cheerful" mean in the sentence below?

> The students were cheerful when their team won the championship.

A upset
B happy
C moody
D jealous

8 What does the word "recently" mean in the sentence below?

> Carla recently went to the dentist to have her teeth cleaned.

A not long ago
B never before
C with concern
D in the afternoon

9 What does the word "sincerely" mean in the sentence below?

> Aunt Martha was sincerely sorry for breaking our new lamp.

A with fear
B with shame
C with honesty
D with concern

10 What does the word "cowardly" mean in the sentence below?

> The story was about a cowardly lion that learned how to be brave.

A in danger
B full of fear
C lacking friends
D with little strength

STOP

Vocabulary   Grade 5, Unit 1: School Spirit!

Name _____ Date _____

Lesson 5
WEEKLY TESTS 5.4

Theme, Selection Test

Elisa's Diary
Comprehension

*D*irections

Think back to the selection "Elisa's Diary" to answer questions 1–10. For each question, circle the letter next to your answer choice.

1 Which of these **best** completes the graphic organizer?

Detail: Elisa is sad.	Detail: Elisa used to live in Puerto Rico.	Detail: Elisa does not understand a lot of English.

Theme:

  A It can be fun to learn new things.
  B It is important to be loyal to friends.
  C It can be helpful to work with other people.
  D It is difficult to adjust to living in a new place.

2 What is different about Elisa staying with her grandmother this time?

  A She is staying by herself with her grandmother.
  B She is helping her grandmother move to a new home.
  C She is living with her grandmother rather than visiting her.
  D She is learning how to take care of the squirrels from her grandmother.

3 Why does Francisco suggest that Elisa watch television?

  A to learn English
  B to learn about football
  C to learn about America
  D to learn how to care for a pet

4 How are José and Elisa alike?

  A They both like to draw pictures.
  B They both like watching squirrels.
  C They are both from another country.
  D They both live with their grandmother.

Comprehension
© Houghton Mifflin Harcourt Publishing Company. All rights reserved.

Grade 5, Unit 1: School Spirit!

Lesson 5
WEEKLY TESTS 5.5

Name _____ Date _____

Elisa's Diary
Comprehension

5 What happened when José told about the customs and traditions of his country?

  A The students clapped.
  B Elisa felt embarrassed.
  C The students mocked him.
  D Elisa volunteered to go next.

6 What was the theme of Elisa's composition?

  A Maya
  B America
  C Guatemala
  D Puerto Rico

7 With whom did Elisa share her composition grade?

  A José
  B Francisco
  C her grandmother
  D her other teachers

8 What deal did José and Elisa make?

  A to be friends forever
  B to learn how to play sports
  C to help each other with their English skills
  D to visit Puerto Rico and Guatemala together

9 What did Elisa learn from José?

  A It takes a special talent to be an artist.
  B Everyone has strengths and weaknesses.
  C People who speak only one language are dumb.
  D It is important for people to laugh at themselves.

10 What is Elisa at the end of the story?

  A a tourist
  B a teacher
  C a grandmother
  D a high school student

Mark Student Reading Level:
____ Independent ____ Instructional ____ Listening

STOP

Comprehension

Lesson 5
WEEKLY TESTS 5.6

Name _____ Date _____

Elisa's Diary
Decoding

Stressed and Unstressed Syllables

*D*irections
Use what you know about stressed and unstressed syllables to read sentences 1–10. Choose the answer that correctly shows which syllable or syllables of the underlined word are stressed. For each question, circle the letter next to your answer choice.

1 You should be <u>loyal</u> to your family.

  A loy • al
  B loy • AL
  C LOY • al
  D LOY • AL

2 The symbol on that bottle means it contains <u>poison</u>.

  A poi • son
  B POI • son
  C poi • SON
  D POI • SON

3 It was 65 degrees in <u>August</u>!

  A Au • gust
  B AU • gust
  C Au • GUST
  D AU • GUST

4 Rudolf bought three paintings at the <u>auction</u>.

  A auc • tion
  B AU • ction
  C AUC • tion
  D au • CTION

5 The <u>royal</u> family includes three dogs.

  A RO • yal
  B ro • YAL
  C ROY • al
  D ROY • AL

6 The boy looked at the ground, waiting for the <u>awkward</u> moment to pass.

  A awk • ward
  B AW • kward
  C AWK • ward
  D AWKW • ard

Decoding
© Houghton Mifflin Harcourt Publishing Company. All rights reserved.

Grade 5, Unit 1: School Spirit!

Name _____ Date _____

Lesson 5
WEEKLY TESTS 5.7

Elisa's Diary
Decoding

7 The leaky <u>faucet</u> kept Mother up all night.

  A fau • cet
  B FA • ucet
  C FAU • cet
  D FAUC • et

8 In the play, the boy played the part of an amusing <u>coward</u>.

  A cow • ard
  B CO • ward
  C COW • ard
  D co • WARD

9 Bert was the first person to get to the top of the <u>tower</u>.

  A tow • ER
  B TO • wer
  C to • WER
  D TOW • er

10 We will <u>announce</u> our arrival with a loud honk of the car horn.

  A A • nnounce
  B AN • nounce
  C an • NOUNCE
  D AN • NOUNCE

STOP

Decoding
© Houghton Mifflin Harcourt Publishing Company. All rights reserved.

Grade 5, Unit 1: School Spirit!

Name _____ Date _____

Lesson 5
WEEKLY TESTS 5.8

Singular and Plural Nouns

Elisa's Diary
Language Arts

Directions
Use what you know about singular and plural nouns to answer questions 1–10. For each question, circle the letter next to your answer choice.

1 Which of the underlined words in this sentence is a SINGULAR noun?

> When the twin volcanoes erupted, they threw ashes into the sky and onto the plants.

A sky
B ashes
C plants
D volcanoes

2 Which of the underlined words in this sentence is a SINGULAR noun?

> The boss took her notes into all of the meetings she attended on Wednesdays.

A boss
B notes
C meetings
D Wednesdays

3 Which of the underlined words in this sentence is a SINGULAR noun?

> There were five deer grazing near the trees when they heard voices by the river.

A deer
B trees
C river
D voices

4 Which of the underlined words in this sentence is a SINGULAR noun?

> The stories in the newspaper were about our brave firefighters and police officers.

A stories
B officers
C newspaper
D firefighters

Language Arts
© Houghton Mifflin Harcourt Publishing Company. All rights reserved.

Grade 5, Unit 1: School Spirit!

Lesson 5
WEEKLY TESTS 5.9

Name _____ Date _____

Elisa's Diary
Language Arts

5 Which of the underlined words in this sentence is a SINGULAR noun?

> The men and women in the camp worked together to put up the tents.

A men
B tents
C camp
D women

6 Which of the underlined words in this sentence is a PLURAL noun?

> In the spring, the shepherd took his sheep up the hill to a large field.

A hill
B field
C sheep
D shepherd

7 Which of the underlined words in this sentence is a PLURAL noun?

> Some people came to the school and left a donation box by the front door.

A box
B door
C school
D people

8 Which of the underlined words in this sentence is a PLURAL noun?

> The city's lights shone brightly on the horizon last night.

A city's
B lights
C night
D horizon

Go On

Language Arts
© Houghton Mifflin Harcourt Publishing Company. All rights reserved.

Grade 5, Unit 1: School Spirit!

Name _____ Date _____

Lesson 5
WEEKLY TESTS 5.10

Elisa's Diary
Language Arts

9 Which of the underlined words in this sentence is a PLURAL noun?

The <u>mice</u> enjoyed eating the <u>cheese</u> as their <u>snack</u> for the <u>day</u>.

A day
B mice
C snack
D cheese

10 Which of the underlined words in this sentence is a PLURAL noun?

<u>Tess</u> tried to collect different colored <u>leaves</u> for her <u>project</u>, but she did not have any <u>luck</u>.

A luck
B Tess
C leaves
D project

STOP

Language Arts

Grade 5, Unit 1: School Spirit!

Name _____ Date _____

Lesson 6
WEEKLY TESTS 6.1

Interrupted Journey
Test Record Form

TEST RECORD FORM	Possible Score	Criterion Score	Student Score
Skills in Context: Comprehension and Vocabulary: Cause and Effect, Target Vocabulary	10	8	
Vocabulary: Target Vocabulary, Context Clues	10	8	
Comprehension: Cause and Effect, Selection Test	10	8	
Decoding: Sound/Spelling Changes	10	8	
Language Arts: Adjectives and Articles	10	8	
TOTAL	40	32	

Total Student Score × 2.5 = _____ %

- -

Test Record Form
© Houghton Mifflin Harcourt Publishing Company. All rights reserved.

Grade 5, Unit 2: Wild Encounters

Lesson 6
WEEKLY TESTS 6.2

Name _____ Date _____

Interrupted Journey
Vocabulary

Target Vocabulary, Antonyms

*D*irections
Use what you know about the target vocabulary and using a thesaurus to answer questions 1–10. For each question, circle the letter next to your answer choice.

1 What does the word "treating" mean in the sentence below?

> The doctor is treating his new patient at the hospital.

A caring for
B paying for
C working for
D traveling for

2 What does the word "analyzing" mean in the sentence below?

> The students were analyzing the results of their experiment.

A studying
B reporting
C balancing
D destroying

3 What does the word "basking" mean in the sentence below?

> The snake was lying on the rock and basking in the sunlight.

A moving quickly
B sleeping quietly
C hiding in shadows
D relaxing in warmth

4 What does the word "marine" mean in the sentence below?

> Arturo wants to study marine life when he goes to college.

A sea
B forest
C desert
D mountain

Go On

Vocabulary
© Houghton Mifflin Harcourt Publishing Company. All rights reserved.

Grade 5, Unit 2: Wild Encounters

Lesson 6
WEEKLY TESTS 6.3

Name _____ Date _____

Interrupted Journey
Vocabulary

5 What does the word "juvenile" mean in the sentence below?

> The juvenile raccoon imitated its mother as she cleaned a fish to eat.

A silly
B brave
C young
D clumsy

6 Read this thesaurus entry for antonyms for the word "ease."

> **ease** *noun*
> Antonyms: difficulty, strife, uneasiness, unrest

Which word from the entry is an antonym for the word "ease" as it is used in the following sentence?

> He opened the jar with great ease.

A strife
B unrest
C difficulty
D uneasiness

7 Read this thesaurus entry for antonyms for the word "public."

> **public** *adjective*
> Antonyms: particular, private, specific, unknown

Which word from the entry is an antonym for the word "public" as it is used in the following sentence?

> The library is a public building.

A private
B specific
C particular
D unknown

8 Read this thesaurus entry for antonyms for the word "perish."

> **perish** *verb*
> Antonyms: breathe, give birth, revive, survive

Which word from the entry is an antonym for the word "perish" as it is used in the following sentence?

> Many animals perish in the harsh desert climate.

A revive
B breathe
C survive
D give birth

Vocabulary

Grade 5, Unit 2: Wild Encounters

Name _____ Date _____

Lesson 6
WEEKLY TESTS 6.4

Interrupted Journey
Vocabulary

9 Read this thesaurus entry for antonyms for the word "observe."

> **observe** *verb*
> Antonyms: break, forget, miss, overlook

Which word from the entry is an antonym for the word "observe" as it is used in the following sentence?

The criminal will observe the law.

A miss
B break
C forget
D overlook

10 Read this thesaurus entry for antonyms for the word "furious."

> **furious** *adjective*
> Antonyms: calm, cheerful, excited, peaceful

Which word from the entry is an antonym for the word "furious" as it is used in the following sentence?

The man was furious about the broken lamp.

A calm
B excited
C cheerful
D peaceful

STOP

Vocabulary
© Houghton Mifflin Harcourt Publishing Company. All rights reserved.

Grade 5, Unit 2: Wild Encounters

Name _____ Date _____

Lesson 6
WEEKLY TESTS 6.5

Cause and Effect, Selection Test

Interrupted Journey
Comprehension

Directions

Think back to the selection "Interrupted Journey: Saving Endangered Sea Turtles" to answer questions 1–10. For each question, circle the letter next to your answer choice.

1 Why does the young sea turtle become confused while swimming?

  A It has too much food to eat.
  B The days begin to lengthen.
  C The water grows colder and colder.
  D The sun no longer shines in the same place.

2 If the sea turtle is not found by volunteers, it will probably

  A die on the beach
  B look for its family
  C swim farther south
  D find a warm shelter

3 What is one effect of the wind on the ocean?

  A It blows warm water.
  B It makes the waves smaller.
  C It causes Max's eyes to water.
  D It forces the ocean to wash over Max.

4 Max and his mother walk on the Cape Cod beach during November and December because

  A it is where the Pilgrims once walked
  B it is the calmest time on the Cape Cod shore
  C that is when sea turtles need help to stay alive
  D they enjoy seeing the snow swirl over the water

5 Max and his mother hunt for sea turtles in order to

  A find turtles to keep as pets
  B capture turtles to give to aquariums
  C count how many turtles died that year
  D save turtles that are threatened or endangered

Comprehension
© Houghton Mifflin Harcourt Publishing Company. All rights reserved.

Grade 5, Unit 2: Wild Encounters

Name _____ Date _____

Lesson 6
WEEKLY TESTS 6.6

Interrupted Journey
Comprehension

6 Why does Max put a stick near the sea turtle?

A to protect the turtle from predators
B to show which direction the wind is blowing
C to let the turtle know it is on land when it wakes up
D to mark the spot where the turtle is for the rescue team

7 What happens **right after** Max sees the turtle move in the wading pool?

A The turtle is returned to the ocean.
B The team is convinced the turtle is still alive.
C The team lowers the temperature of the turtle.
D A veterinarian listens closely for the turtle's heartbeat.

8 A sign that the turtle is dead would be

A wide-open eyes
B dried and wrinkled limbs
C a slow but steady heartbeat
D a temperature above 50 degrees Fahrenheit

9 Why do guests at the Hidden Harbor Motel stay out of the swimming pool?

A The pool has no water.
B The pool is full of sea turtles.
C Guests can swim in the nearby ocean.
D Guests would have to pay extra to swim.

10 By setting the turtle free in a cove, Richie Moretti hopes the turtle will

A learn how to avoid fishing nets
B have the best chance of survival
C find a home and stay in the cove
D be around tourists and entertain them

Mark Student Reading Level:

____ Independent ____ Instructional ____ Listening

STOP

Comprehension

© Houghton Mifflin Harcourt Publishing Company. All rights reserved.

Grade 5, Unit 2: Wild Encounters

Lesson 6
WEEKLY TESTS 6.7

Name _____ Date _____

Common Beginning Syllables

Interrupted Journey
Decoding

Directions
Use what you know about common beginning syllables to answer questions 1–10. Choose the words that best complete the sentences. For each question, circle the letter next to your answer choice.

1 The shop was so busy that the owner hired an

  A ipprentice
  B upprentice
  C epprentice
  D apprentice

2 The dog was rewarded for its good

  A bihavior
  B behavior
  C bahavior
  D buhavior

3 The science lesson is very

  A camplicated
  B complicated
  C cumplicated
  D coumplicated

4 Last week, my father went to Ohio for a

  A canvention
  B cunvention
  C convention
  D caenvention

5 It is taking the jury a long time to make a

  A dicision
  B dacision
  C decision
  D ducision

6 The teacher gave her students a very nice

  A campliment
  B cumpliment
  C compliment
  D coumpliment

Decoding
© Houghton Mifflin Harcourt Publishing Company. All rights reserved.

Grade 5, Unit 2: Wild Encounters

Name _____ Date _____

Lesson 6
WEEKLY TESTS 6.8

Interrupted Journey
Decoding

7 The store owner hopes this month's sales will

A increase
B encrease
C ancrease
D uncrease

8 Due to the bad weather, the builders have made very little

A pragress
B progress
C prowgress
D prawgress

9 We did not hear the mayor's

A rumark
B remark
C ramark
D reimark

10 The young girl stood on the stage and sang with

A canfidence
B confidence
C coinfidence
D caenfidence

STOP

Decoding
© Houghton Mifflin Harcourt Publishing Company. All rights reserved.

Grade 5, Unit 2: Wild Encounters

Name _____ Date _____

Lesson 6
WEEKLY TESTS 6.9

Verbs

Interrupted Journey
Language Arts

Directions
Use what you know about verbs to answer questions 1–10. For each question, circle the letter next to your answer choice.

1. Which word in the sentence is a VERB?

    Aunt Lorraine runs in the park every day.

    A Lorraine
    B runs
    C park
    D every

2. Which word in the sentence is a VERB?

    Every week, Nathan writes a story in his journal.

    A Every
    B Nathan
    C writes
    D his

3. Which word in the sentence is a VERB?

    Eliza and Peter usually ride horses at their grandfather's ranch.

    A and
    B usually
    C ride
    D horses

4. Which word in the sentence is a VERB?

    Every morning, I listen to music on the radio.

    A Every
    B morning
    C I
    D listen

5. Which words in the sentence are VERBS?

    Carson will study all night for his science test.

    A will study
    B all night
    C for his
    D science test

Language Arts
© Houghton Mifflin Harcourt Publishing Company. All rights reserved.

Grade 5, Unit 2: Wild Encounters

Lesson 6
WEEKLY TESTS 6.10

Name _____ Date _____

Interrupted Journey
Language Arts

6 Which word in the sentence is a VERB?

> The baseball flew across the field and through the window of the old shed.

A baseball
B flew
C through
D shed

7 Which word in the sentence is a VERB?

> Coach Myers waved his arms in excitement.

A Myers
B waved
C his
D excitement

8 Which words in the sentence are VERBS?

> The hikers, a group of students from the city, were enjoying the scenery along the forest trail.

A The hikers
B from the city
C were enjoying
D scenery along the

9 Which word in the sentence is a VERB?

> The twins ate trail mix for their snack.

A twins
B ate
C mix
D snack

10 Which words in the sentence are VERBS?

> George is washing the dirty dishes from this morning's breakfast.

A is washing
B dirty dishes
C from this
D morning's breakfast

STOP

Language Arts
© Houghton Mifflin Harcourt Publishing Company. All rights reserved.

Grade 5, Unit 2: Wild Encounters

Name _____ Date _____

Lesson 7
WEEKLY TESTS 7.1

Old Yeller
Test Record Form

TEST RECORD FORM	Possible Score	Criterion Score	Student Score
Vocabulary: Target Vocabulary, Idioms (Adages & Common Sayings)	10	8	
Comprehension: Understanding Characters, Selection Test	10	8	
Decoding: Vowel + /r/ Sounds	10	8	
Language Arts: Direct and Indirect Objects	10	8	
TOTAL	40	32	

Total Student Score × 2.5 = _____ %

Test Record Form
© Houghton Mifflin Harcourt Publishing Company. All rights reserved.

Grade 5, Unit 2: Wild Encounters

Lesson 7
WEEKLY TESTS 7.2

Name _____ Date _____

Old Yeller
Vocabulary

Target Vocabulary, Idioms (Adages & Common Sayings)

Directions
Use what you know about the target vocabulary and idioms to answer questions 1–10. For each question, circle the letter next to your answer choice.

1 What does the word "frantic" mean in the sentence below?

> The engineer was frantic when he discovered that the brakes on the train did not work.

A lazy
B brave
C jealous
D fearful

2 What does the word "stride" mean in the sentence below?

> The turtle has a slow stride.

A step
B brain
C voice
D dream

3 What does the word "bounding" mean in the sentence below?

> The children went bounding out the door to the playground.

A taking away
B settling down
C walking around
D leaping forward

4 What does the word "strained" mean in the sentence below?

> The farmer strained to lift the giant pumpkin.

A tried to avoid
B stood one's ground
C answered one's calling
D stretched one's muscles

Go On

Vocabulary
© Houghton Mifflin Harcourt Publishing Company. All rights reserved.

Grade 5, Unit 2: Wild Encounters

Lesson 7
WEEKLY TESTS 7.3

Old Yeller
Vocabulary

5 What does the word "picturing" mean in the sentence below?

The boy was picturing where to bury his treasure.

A making a mental image
B drawing a detailed map
C writing directions on paper
D discussing possible locations

6 What does this sentence mean?

Dawn wracked her brain to remember where her keys were.

A Dawn thought hard to remember where her keys were.
B Dawn drew a picture to remember where her keys were.
C Dawn tapped her head to remember where her keys were.
D Dawn made a mental image to remember where her keys were.

7 What does this sentence mean?

Making a kite was as easy as pie.

A Making a kite was simple.
B Making a kite was difficult.
C Making a kite took patience.
D Making a kite took several steps.

8 What does this sentence mean?

Kelsey is comparing apples and oranges.

A Kelsey is comparing herself to others.
B Kelsey is comparing different types of fruit.
C Kelsey is comparing items that are the same.
D Kelsey is comparing two completely different things.

Lesson 7
WEEKLY TESTS 7.4

Name _____   Date _____

Old Yeller
Vocabulary

9 What does this sentence mean?

Mara won the race by the skin of her teeth.

A Mara just barely won the race.
B Mara won the race by cheating.
C Mara won the race by a long distance.
D Mara won the race despite being injured.

10 What does this sentence mean?

Toby cleaned his room with a lick and a promise.

A Toby never cleaned his room.
B Toby cleaned his room in a rush.
C Toby said he would clean his room.
D Toby did a thorough job cleaning his room.

STOP

Vocabulary

Grade 5, Unit 2: Wild Encounters

Name _____ Date _____

Lesson 7
WEEKLY TESTS 7.5

Understanding Characters, Selection Test

Old Yeller
Comprehension

Directions
Think back to the selection "Old Yeller" to answer questions 1–10. For each question, circle the letter next to your answer choice.

1 Sweat pours off Travis and his muscles ache so badly he can barely lift the axe because he is

A so lazy
B in the sun
C working hard
D smaller than the axe

2 What does the description of Little Arliss as "a screamer by nature" tell the reader?

A Little Arliss is a noisy child.
B Little Arliss is too young to talk.
D Travis screams at Little Arliss every day.
C People talk to Little Arliss by screaming.

3 Travis is too tired to split more fence rails, but he races through the woods to help Little Arliss because

A Little Arliss is calling for him
B he wants Little Arliss to stop screaming
C he is frightened and worried about Little Arliss
D his mother shouts that Little Arliss is in trouble

4 How are Little Arliss and the bear cub alike?

A They are both screamers.
B They are both frightened.
C They both are in the water.
D They both have hold of each other.

Comprehension
© Houghton Mifflin Harcourt Publishing Company. All rights reserved.

Grade 5, Unit 2: Wild Encounters

Name _____ Date _____

Lesson 7
WEEKLY TESTS 7.6

Old Yeller
Comprehension

5 When Travis says, "My heart went pushing up into my throat, nearly choking off my wind," the reader can tell that Travis

A feels afraid
B is energized
C runs very fast
D is getting sick

6 How does the mother bear feel when she hears her cub whimpering?

A sad
B tired
C angry
D curious

7 The reader can tell that Mama

A will kill the bear
B is a brave person
C is away from home
D will save Little Arliss

8 The stray dog gets the name Old Yeller because he is

A old
B noisy
C brave
D yellow

9 Why does Travis decide to take good care of Old Yeller?

A because Little Arliss asks him to
B because Old Yeller saves Little Arliss
C because Papa is driving cattle to market
D because the dog is hurt by the mother bear

10 At the end of the story, Travis realizes that

A Little Arliss is a troublemaker
B he loves Little Arliss more than he knew
C he should always pay attention to Little Arliss's screams
D his mother loves Little Arliss more than she loves Travis

Mark Student Reading Level:

____ Independent   ____ Instructional   ____ Listening

STOP

Comprehension

Grade 5, Unit 2: Wild Encounters

Name _____ Date _____

Lesson 7
WEEKLY TESTS 7.7

Vowel + /r/ Sounds

Old Yeller
Decoding

*D*irections
Use what you know about vowel + /r/ sounds to complete the sentence in questions 1–10. For each question, circle the letter next to your answer choice.

1 The land is not as flat as it

   A   apears
   B   appaers
   C   appears
   D   appeers

2 After a long day at work, Don felt

   A   wary
   B   waery
   C   weary
   D   weery

3 You must plan ahead for your future

   A   carrer
   B   carear
   C   career
   D   carrier

4 During a test, it is important to stay

   A   alirt
   B   alert
   C   alurt
   D   alort

5 My mother is a hospital

   A   voluntir
   B   volunteir
   C   voluntear
   D   volunteer

6 Last year, Nora went to Japan as a

   A   turist
   B   torist
   C   teurist
   D   tourist

- -

Decoding
© Houghton Mifflin Harcourt Publishing Company. All rights reserved.

Grade 5, Unit 2: Wild Encounters

Lesson 7
WEEKLY TESTS 7.8

Name _____ Date _____

Old Yeller
Decoding

7 To back up, put the car in

   A revirse
   B reverse
   C revarse
   D revurse

8 Every morning, the rooster crows very

   A airly
   B eirly
   C early
   D eerly

9 It is difficult to swim against the

   A curant
   B current
   C currant
   D currint

10 The day was dark and

   A driery
   B dreery
   C draery
   D dreary

STOP

Decoding

© Houghton Mifflin Harcourt Publishing Company. All rights reserved.

Grade 5, Unit 2: Wild Encounters

Lesson 7
WEEKLY TESTS 7.9

Name _____ Date _____

Direct and Indirect Objects

Old Yeller
Language Arts

*D*irections
Use what you know about direct and indirect objects to answer questions 1–10. For each question, circle the letter next to your answer choice.

1 Which of the underlined words is a DIRECT OBJECT?

Erica is climbing the steepest trail.

A Erica
B climbing
C steepest
D trail

2 Which of the underlined words is a DIRECT OBJECT?

The teacher is judging the art competition.

A teacher
B is
C art
D competition

3 Which of the underlined words is a DIRECT OBJECT?

The sisters can watch several movies without getting tired.

A watch
B movies
C without
D tired

4 Which of the underlined words is a DIRECT OBJECT?

George will finish the painting this evening.

A will
B finish
C painting
D evening

Language Arts
© Houghton Mifflin Harcourt Publishing Company. All rights reserved.

Grade 5, Unit 2: Wild Encounters

Name _____ Date _____

Lesson 7
WEEKLY TESTS 7.10

Old Yeller
Language Arts

5 Which words are a COMPOUND DIRECT OBJECT?

> Mom and Dad bought some apples and oranges at the grocery store.

A Mom and Dad
B bought some
C apples and oranges
D the grocery store

6 Which words are a COMPOUND DIRECT OBJECT?

> On Friday and Saturday, my brother and I had fun playing basketball and baseball.

A Friday and Saturday
B my brother and I
C had fun playing
D basketball and baseball

7 Which words are a COMPOUND DIRECT OBJECT?

> The football coach explained the rules and regulations of the game.

A football coach
B explained the
C rules and regulations
D of the game

8 Which of the underlined words is an INDIRECT OBJECT?

> The judge gave Alice a gold medal for winning the swimming race.

A judge
B Alice
C medal
D race

Go On

Language Arts
© Houghton Mifflin Harcourt Publishing Company. All rights reserved.

Grade 5, Unit 2: Wild Encounters

Lesson 7
WEEKLY TESTS 7.11

Old Yeller
Language Arts

9 Which of the underlined words is an INDIRECT OBJECT?

The <u>farmer</u> and <u>her daughters</u> sold the <u>market</u> their entire corn <u>harvest</u>.

A farmer
B her daughters
C market
D harvest

10 Which of the underlined words is an INDIRECT OBJECT?

<u>Mr. Fitzgerald</u> and <u>his fifth-grade class</u> <u>sent</u> <u>their principal</u> a giant get-well soon card.

A Mr. Fitzgerald
B his fifth-grade class
C sent
D their principal

STOP

Language Arts
Grade 5, Unit 2: Wild Encounters

Name _____ Date _____

Lesson 8
WEEKLY TESTS 8.1

Riding Freedom
Test Record Form

TEST RECORD FORM	Possible Score	Criterion Score	Student Score
Skills in Context: Persuasion, Target Vocabulary	10	8	
Vocabulary: Target Vocabulary, Prefixes *en-*, *re-*, *pre-*, *pro-*	10	8	
Comprehension: Persuasion, Selection Test	10	8	
Decoding: Homophones	10	8	
Language Arts: Conjunctions	10	8	
TOTAL	50	42	
		Total Student Score × 2 =	%

Go On

Test Record Form
© Houghton Mifflin Harcourt Publishing Company. All rights reserved.

Grade 5, Unit 2: Wild Encounters

Name _____ Date _____

Persuasion, Target Vocabulary

Everglades Forever
Skills in Context

***D**irections*
Read the selection. Then read each question that follows the selection. Decide which is the best answer to each question. For each question, circle the letter next to your answer choice.

Dolan Falls Preserve

Come and explore the Dolan Falls Preserve! It is one of the most beautiful places in Texas! The preserve is located where a plateau, a desert, and a brushland meet. A plateau is a raised, flat piece of land. A desert is a place that gets little or no rain. A brushland is covered with plants that do not grow very high. The sparkling waters of the Devils River, Dolan Springs, and Dolan Creek are located in this <u>unique</u> place. The preserve also has a wide variety of plants and animals.

The Devils River is about fifty miles long and, in some places, it flows under the ground. There is a wetland along the river. The dirt is rich and wet. Many plants grow in the fresh water and along the river banks. Not far from the wetlands, the land turns very dry. Desert plants, such as cactus, grow in the dry land.

Dolan Falls is in the middle of the preserve. It is not far from where the Devils River and Dolan Creek meet. At Dolan Falls, the water rushes over eight feet of rocky ledges. To the west of the falls, there is a forest with many kinds of trees. A pretty bush, called the Texas Snowbell, thrives along Dolan Creek. The bush blooms in April and May and has groups of white flowers with five long, thin petals. Its leaves are shaped like a circle. Under the leaves there are silver hairs.

There are many animals that live within the preserve, including fish, lizards, and turtles. Some birds and butterflies stop along the Devils River during their migration south for the winter. The black-capped vireo, which is a type of songbird, and the monarch butterfly make this trip every year. The black-capped vireo is small. The male has black feathers on his head, which is how the bird gets its name, and white

Name _____ **Date** _____

Lesson 8
WEEKLY TESTS 8.3

Everglades Forever
Skills in Context

around its red eyes, so it looks like it is wearing glasses. Its wings and back are dark green, but the wings have yellow bars on them. The females and babies have gray feathers on their head and brown eyes. Monarchs are orange, black, and white. They cannot live in cold weather, so millions of them fly up to 3,000 miles to stay warm during the winter months.

Long ago, Native Americans lived on the land that is now the preserve. Many different groups lived here. Some built their homes with rocks. They drew pictures on the rocks, which show what their lives were like. In 1590, the first explorers traveled up the Devils River. Then, about 300 years later, the first settlers built a ranch along the river.

In 1991, a group called the Nature Conservancy took on the responsibility of protecting Dolan Falls Preserve. The group believed that the freshwater springs that flowed into the Devils River and Dolan Creek needed protection. The group also believed that some of the plants and animals were endangered. Because there were few of them left alive, it was important to keep them safe. Today, the Nature Conservancy keeps track of the number of plants and animals within the preserve and makes sure that people do not harm them. The Nature Conservancy limits the number of people who come to the preserve by keeping it closed most of the time. People are allowed to visit the preserve on field trips and to help on workdays. As long as it is protected, Dolan Falls Preserve will always be a place of beauty.

---

1 Which sentence is used to persuade the reader to read this selection?

 A *A plateau is a raised, flat piece of land.*
 B *It is one of the most beautiful places in Texas!*
 C *The preserve also has a wide variety of plants and animals.*
 D *The preserve is located where a plateau, a desert, and a brushland meet.*

2 What does the word "unique" mean as it is used in the first paragraph?

 A wet
 B lovely
 C one of a kind
 D out of the way

Go On

Skills in Context
© Houghton Mifflin Harcourt Publishing Company. All rights reserved.

Grade 5, Unit 2: Wild Encounters

Lesson 8
WEEKLY TESTS 8.4

Name _____ Date _____

Everglades Forever
Skills in Context

3 Where is Dolan Falls located?

A It is in the desert.
B It is in a wetland along the river.
C It is in the middle of the preserve.
D It is far from where the Devils River and Dolan Creek meet.

4 How are black-capped vireos and monarch butterflies alike?

A They both live at the preserve all year long.
B They are both types of birds with black feathers.
C They were both kept as pets by Native Americans.
D They both stop along the Devils River in the winter.

5 What happened in 1590?

A The first settlers built a ranch along the Devils River.
B The first explorers traveled up the Devils River.
C The Nature Conservancy took over the preserve.
D The first Texas snowbell grew along Dolan Creek.

6 Why is the Nature Conservancy important?

A It builds ranches for settlers.
B It protects the Dolan Falls Preserve.
C It changes the desert land into wetlands.
D It plants Texas Snowbells along Dolan Creek.

Lesson 8
WEEKLY TESTS 8.5

Name _____ Date _____

Everglades Forever
Skills in Context

7 Which words in the sixth paragraph help the reader know what "endangered" means?

   A keeps track of the number
   B living things stay healthy
   C some of the plants and animals
   D there were few of them left alive

8 People are not allowed to enter the preserve whenever they want to because they might

   A dig for gold and silver
   B swim in the Dolan Creek
   C harm the plants and animals
   D build factories that pollute the water

9 Which sentence from the selection persuades the reader to think about the future of Dolan Falls Preserve?

   A They do this by keeping the preserve closed most of the time.
   B The group keeps track of the number of plants and animals.
   C People are invited to come for field trips and to help on workdays.
   D As long as it is protected, Doland Falls Preserve will always be a place of beauty.

10 Why did the author write this selection?

   A to compare the preserve to other beautiful places in nature
   B to describe how the waterfalls in the preserve were created
   C to entertain the reader with an exciting story about the preserve
   D to convince the reader that the preserve needs to be protected

STOP

Skills in Context

Grade 5, Unit 2: Wild Encounters

Target Vocabulary, Prefixes en-, re-, pre-, pro-

Everglades Forever
Vocabulary

Directions
Use what you know about the target vocabulary and prefixes to answer questions 1–10. For each question, circle the letter next to your answer choice.

1 What does the word "conserving" mean in the sentence below?

> During the drought, we will be conserving water.

A saving
B licensing
C condensing
D transporting

2 What does the word "vegetation" mean in the sentence below?

> The mountains are covered with different kinds of vegetation.

A plants
B water
C outfits
D vessels

3 What does the word "restore" mean in the sentence below?

> The electric company worked hard to restore power to the homes.

A repay
B return
C reflect
D release

4 What does the word "attracted" mean in the sentence below?

> The butterflies are attracted to the sweet-smelling flowers.

A drawn to
B perched on
C worked with
D frightened by

Vocabulary

Grade 5, Unit 2: Wild Encounters

Name _____ Date _____

Lesson 8
WEEKLY TESTS 8.7

Everglades Forever
Vocabulary

5 What does the word "regulate" mean in the sentence below?

> The rangers regulate activities within the park.

A want
B invite
C control
D discourage

6 What does the word "review" mean in the sentence below?

> Dawn will review the materials for the test.

A look over again
B look over before
C look over carefully
D look over for the first time

7 What does the word "predetermined" mean in the sentence below?

> The outcome of the race was predetermined.

A never decided
B too close to decide
C decided afterwards
D decided ahead of time

8 What does the word "enclose" mean in the sentence below?

> April will enclose the garden with a fence.

A close in
B close later
C close before
D close tightly

9 What does the word "proceed" mean in the sentence below?

> The police officer told us to proceed carefully.

A move slowly
B move quickly
C move forward
D move backward

10 What does the word "predates" mean in the sentence below?

> The law predates your birth.

A comes after
B comes too late
C comes before
D comes early

STOP

Vocabulary

Grade 5, Unit 2: Wild Encounters

Name _____ Date _____

Lesson 8
WEEKLY TESTS 8.8

Everglades Forever
Comprehension

Persuasion, Selection Test

Directions
Think back to the selection "Everglades Forever: Restoring America's Great Wetland" to answer questions 1–10. For each question, circle the letter next to your answer choice.

1. People could persuade others to support the work of the Comprehensive Everglades Restoration Plan by

   A   telling them the rules
   B   showing them a map of the area
   C   creating a smaller group to feed the animals
   D   taking them to visit the wetland so they can see it themselves

2. Why does Ms. Stone get a park ranger to talk to the class?

   A   to teach them about wetlands
   B   to entertain them with animal stories
   C   to persuade them to join the Restoration Plan
   D   to help them identify birds and trees by name

3. What argument does the author give for keeping mangrove swamps alive?

   A   Rainwater mixes with salty ocean water.
   B   Fish migrate to deep water to look for food.
   C   The water spreads out the food that animals eat.
   D   Their waters protect young animals as they grow up.

4. How does Ranger Jim help persuade students that it is important to save the Everglades?

   A   He tells them that human, animal, and plant life are all connected.
   B   He tells them that they will see animals together around deep water.
   C   He tells them that alligators use their bodies to dig deep holes for water.
   D   He tells them that bark peels off the tourist tree like skin off sunburned people.

Comprehension
© Houghton Mifflin Harcourt Publishing Company. All rights reserved.

Grade 5, Unit 2: Wild Encounters

Name _____ Date _____

Lesson 8
WEEKLY TESTS 8.9

Everglades Forever
Comprehension

5 People will **best** be convinced to conserve water if they read that

A *there is a deep part of the slough at the beginning of the trail*
B *most of the water used in southern Florida comes from the Everglades*
C *the landscape changes from houses and shopping centers to a flat, grassy prairie*
D *differences in moisture help create unique habitats, each with its own special set of plants and animals*

6 One reason given for saving the sawgrass prairie is

A silence
B growth
C marshes
D development

7 After the students see the many habitats of the Everglades, they

A are against farming and development
B support development in the Everglades
C are against harming life in the Everglades
D support farming and are against development

8 What does the author believe about saving the Everglades?

A It must be done to preserve all life on Earth.
B People can do it if they start now and work hard.
C Finger glades are the most important parts to save.
D The government is responsible for saving everything.

Mark Student Reading Level:
____ Independent   ____ Instructional   ____ Listening

Go On

Comprehension
© Houghton Mifflin Harcourt Publishing Company. All rights reserved.

Grade 5, Unit 2: Wild Encounters

Everglades Forever
Comprehension

9 Students in southern Florida can help save the Everglades by

A deciding to become part of the circle of life
B persuading their families to use less water in their homes
C living however they choose today and not worrying about tomorrow
D telling people that they are responsible for protecting alligators

10 Which sentence from the selection shows that the students truly learn the value of the Everglades?

A *Small animals live, feed, and raise their young in the solution holes.*
B *Restoring the Everglades will take a long time, and it may never be finished.*
C *But now the ground, which is higher than the larger sawgrass prairies, was dry and hard.*
D *They had learned that they too were a part of the Everglades, connected in the same circle of life with the tiniest insect and largest alligator.*

STOP

Lesson 8
WEEKLY TESTS 8.11

Name _____ Date _____

Everglades Forever
Decoding

Homophones

Directions
Use what you know about homophones to complete the sentence in questions 1–10. For each question, circle the letter next to your answer choice.

1 The scratch on my hand took three days to _____.

  A hele
  B heal
  C heel
  D he'll

2 I hammered the nail into the _____.

  A board
  B bored
  C boared
  D boored

3 Our dance teacher told us to _____ partners.

  A chose
  B chews
  C choose
  D chooze

4 The letter we _____ yesterday came back today.

  A sint
  B sent
  C cent
  D scent

5 All day Jennifer walked around in a _____.

  A dais
  B dase
  C days
  D daze

6 I would like to eat a _____.

  A pair
  B pare
  C pear
  D peer

Go On

Decoding
© Houghton Mifflin Harcourt Publishing Company. All rights reserved.

Grade 5, Unit 2: Wild Encounters

Name _____ Date _____

Lesson 8
WEEKLY TESTS 8.12

Everglades Forever
Decoding

7 The _____ to the throne was about to speak to the crowd.

- **A** air
- **B** err
- **C** hair
- **D** heir

8 We went to the store to _____ some groceries.

- **A** bi
- **B** by
- **C** buy
- **D** bye

9 The bride was walking down the _____.

- **A** ill
- **B** I'll
- **C** isle
- **D** aisle

10 Stop crunching so loudly on that _____!

- **A** carat
- **B** caret
- **C** karat
- **D** carrot

STOP

Decoding

Grade 5, Unit 2: Wild Encounters

Name _____ Date _____

Conjunctions

Lesson 8
WEEKLY TESTS 8.13

Everglades Forever
Language Arts

Directions
Use what you know about conjunctions to answer questions 1–10. For each question, circle the letter next to your answer choice.

1 Which conjunction **best** completes the sentence?

> The volcano showed signs of being active, _____ some people refused to leave their homes.

A or
B yet
C and
D because

2 Which conjunction **best** completes the sentence?

> _____ Maria worked in the garden, she walked her dog.

A If
B After
C Where
D Because

3 Which conjunction **best** completes the sentence?

> We can play a game, _____ we can paint a picture.

A or
B so
C but
D while

4 Which conjunction **best** completes the sentence?

> Tommy would take Ann to the bus, _____ that would make him late for work.

A since
B while
C but
D because

Go On

Language Arts
© Houghton Mifflin Harcourt Publishing Company. All rights reserved.

Grade 5, Unit 2: Wild Encounters

Name _____ Date _____

Lesson 8
WEEKLY TESTS 8.14

Everglades Forever
Language Arts

5 Which conjunction **best** completes the sentence?

   _____ Craig already had his ticket, he still had to wait in line to see the movie.

   A Yet
   B Unless
   C Because
   D Although

6 Which conjunction **best** completes the sentence?

   I wanted to learn about stars, _____ I did some research at the library.

   A so
   B or
   C but
   D yet

7 Which conjunction **best** completes the sentence?

   Julie took an umbrella to school _____ it looked like it might rain.

   A so
   B but
   C although
   D because

8 Which conjunction **best** completes the sentence?

   Did you want vanilla, chocolate, _____ both kinds of ice cream?

   A or
   B so
   C yet
   D nor

9 Which sentence is written correctly?

   A I like dogs cats, and horses.
   B I like dogs: cats and horses.
   C I like dogs, cats, and horses.
   D I like: dogs; cats; and horses.

10 Which sentence is written correctly?

   A Dad wrote these items on the grocery list apple; oranges; and pears.
   B Dad wrote these items on the grocery list: apples oranges and pears.
   C Dad wrote these items on the grocery list: apples, oranges, and pears.
   D Dad wrote these items on the grocery list: apples; oranges; and pears.

STOP

Name _____ Date _____

Lesson 9
WEEKLY TESTS 9.1

Storm Warriors
Test Record Form

TEST RECORD FORM	Possible Score	Criterion Score	Student Score
Vocabulary: Target Vocabulary, Greek and Latin Roots (Greek = *tele*, *photo*; Latin = *scrib*, *rupt*)	10	8	
Comprehension: Conclusions and Generalizations, Selection Test	10	8	
Decoding: Compound Words	10	8	
Language Arts: Complex Sentences	10	8	
TOTAL	40	32	

Total Student Score × 2.5 = _____ %

Go On

Test Record Form
© Houghton Mifflin Harcourt Publishing Company. All rights reserved.

Grade 5, Unit 2: Wild Encounters

Name _____ Date _____

Lesson 9
WEEKLY TESTS 9.2

Storm Warriors
Vocabulary

Target Vocabulary, Greek and Latin Roots (Greek = tele, photo; Latin = scrib, rupt)

Directions
Use what you know about the target vocabulary and Greek and Latin roots to answer questions 1–10. For each question, circle the letter next to your answer choice.

1 What does the word "clammy" mean in the sentence below?

   The sick girl's hands felt cold and clammy.

   A dry
   B sticky
   C crusty
   D graceful

2 What does the word "secured" mean in the sentence below?

   While in the car, the child was secured with a special car seat.

   A held tightly
   B slept quietly
   C affected quickly
   D released recently

3 What does the word "squalling" mean in the sentence below?

   The hungry baby was squalling for her bottle.

   A pointing
   B grabbing
   C laughing
   D screaming

4 What does the word "critical" mean in the sentence below?

   The news report gave critical information about the upcoming election.

   A vital
   B delicate
   C confusing
   D reasonable

- -

Vocabulary
© Houghton Mifflin Harcourt Publishing Company. All rights reserved.

Grade 5, Unit 2: Wild Encounters

Name _____ Date _____

Lesson 9
WEEKLY TESTS 9.3

Storm Warriors
Vocabulary

5 What does the word "demolished" mean in the sentence below?

> The old building was demolished by the bulldozer.

A invented
B furnished
C destroyed
D manufactured

6 Which word **best** completes this sentence?

> Evan took the _____ with his new camera.

A fotograph
B photgraph
C footograph
D photograph

7 Which word **best** completes this sentence?

> Jamie did not mean to _____ the conversation her parents were having.

A interrpt
B interrapt
C interrupt
D interoupt

8 Which word **best** completes this sentence?

> Alberto tried to _____ the beautiful scenery he had seen on his vacation.

A describe
B deskribe
C descrieb
D descrybe

9 Which word **best** completes this sentence?

> Uncle Steven answered the _____.

A telephone
B telaphone
C tellephone
D telluphone

10 Which word **best** completes this sentence?

> The volcano will _____ before morning.

A erupt
B errupt
C eruped
D erupped

STOP

Vocabulary
© Houghton Mifflin Harcourt Publishing Company. All rights reserved.

Grade 5, Unit 2: Wild Encounters

Name _____ Date _____

Lesson 9
WEEKLY TESTS 9.4

Storm Warriors
Comprehension

Conclusions and Generalizations, Selection Test

*D*irections

Think back to the selection "Storm Warriors" to answer questions 1–10. For each question, circle the letter next to your answer choice.

1 After reading the first paragraph of the selection, you can tell that the narrator is

A on a boat
B in the water
C in the building
D on the shore during a storm

2 What conclusion can you draw from the following comment by the narrator?

> "It was unthinkable, what these men were doing. Violence swirled around us—a deadly, churning mix of wind and sea. And these two surfmen were walking *into* it."

A The narrator thinks the surfmen are foolish.
B The narrator thinks the surfmen are in serious danger.
C The narrator thinks the surfmen will fail to save the ship's crew.
D The narrator thinks the ship's crew will save the surfmen's lives.

3 The ship's crew believes that

A women and children should be saved first
B the surfmen should have been able to save their ship
C the captain should have been the last one to leave the ship
D Nathan saved all their lives because of his medical knowledge

4 You can infer that the child is frightened because he

A is wet and shivering
B gets wrapped in a warm blanket
C clings tightly to the narrator's neck
D cries more softly as the narrator holds him

Comprehension
© Houghton Mifflin Harcourt Publishing Company. All rights reserved.

Grade 5, Unit 2: Wild Encounters

Lesson 9
WEEKLY TESTS 9.5

Name _____ Date _____

Storm Warriors
Comprehension

5 When Nathan says, "Treat the bleeding first, then the hypothermia," you can tell that Nathan

   A likes to give orders
   B wishes he were a surfman
   C is studying to become a doctor
   D knows some medical information

6 You can tell that Nathan

   A is a coward
   B likes to help people
   C feels helpless during the rescue
   D blames himself for the sailor's injury

7 How does Nathan **most likely** feel after the rescue?

   A ashamed that he is not a surfman
   B proud that he is learning important things
   C hopeful that he will learn to become a sea captain
   D scared that he will get stuck in a violent storm again

8 What conclusion can you draw about Mrs. Gardiner?

   A She is helpless in an emergency.
   B She has a special relationship with the captain.
   C She has more medical knowledge than Nathan.
   D She is more concerned about herself than about others.

9 What will **most likely** happen after the last paragraph in the story?

   A Everyone will get safely back to the station.
   B The surfmen will return to the ocean to save the ship.
   C The storm will keep the people stranded on the shore.
   D Nathan will decide to work harder to become a surfman.

10 What can you infer about Nathan after reading the story?

   A He is going to study medicine.
   B He will become a brave surfman.
   C He is not sure what his career will be.
   D He will not continue to rescue ship crews.

Mark Student Reading Level:
____ Independent ____ Instructional ____ Listening

STOP

Comprehension
© Houghton Mifflin Harcourt Publishing Company. All rights reserved.

Grade 5, Unit 2: Wild Encounters

Name _____ Date _____

Lesson 9
WEEKLY TESTS 9.6

Compound Words

Storm Warriors
Decoding

Directions
Use what you know about compound words to replace the underlined words in sentences 1–10. For each question, circle the letter next to your answer choice.

1. My father took a <u>tool that shines light</u> on our night hike.

   A flashlite
   B flashlight
   C flash light
   D flash-light

2. The parking spot was reserved for people who used <u>chairs with large wheels</u>.

   A wheelchairs
   B wheel-chairs
   C wheeledchairs
   D wheeled chairs

3. The jungle is full of <u>wild animals and plants</u>.

   A wilelife
   B wildlife
   C wild life
   D wildlives

4. I have a <u>terrible pain in my head</u>, so I am going to lie down.

   A headach
   B headache
   C head ache
   D head-ache

5. I have a <u>part of the week</u> job at the restaurant.

   A partime
   B parttime
   C part time
   D part-time

6. I am going <u>to a country across the sea</u>.

   A overseas
   B overseize
   C over seas
   D over-seas

Decoding
© Houghton Mifflin Harcourt Publishing Company. All rights reserved.

Grade 5, Unit 2: Wild Encounters

Lesson 9
WEEKLY TESTS 9.7

Name _____ Date _____

Storm Warriors
Decoding

7 The lifeguard grabbed the buoyant device designed to keep a person afloat in water and ran.

A lifepreserver
B life preserver
C life-preserver
D live preserver

8 Although it was dark, I knew there was some person in the room.

A somebody
B somebodie
C some-body
D some bodie

9 I will be grateful for eternity if you help me.

A forever
B forevor
C forrever
D forrevor

10 Cindy did not have the most recent schedule.

A uptodate
B up to date
C up-to-date
D up-two-date

STOP

Decoding

Grade 5, Unit 2: Wild Encounters

Complex Sentences

Storm Warriors
Language Arts

Directions
Use what you know about the complex sentences to answer questions 1–10. For each question, circle the letter next to your answer choice.

1 What is the **best** way to combine these sentences?

> **The girls wore mittens. It was cold.**

A The girls wore mittens that were cold.
B The girls wore mittens, so it was cold.
C It was cold, the girls also wore mittens.
D The girls wore mittens because it was cold.

2 What is the **best** way to combine these sentences?

> **Hedda liked playing football. It was her favorite game.**

A Hedda liked playing football, which was her favorite game.
B Hedda's favorite game was because she played football.
C Hedda played football, and football was her favorite game.
D Hedda liked playing football, but it was her favorite game.

3 What is the **best** way to combine these sentences?

> **The baby cried. He was sad because his toy broke.**

A The baby was sad and he cried and this was because his toy broke.
B The baby's sad toy broke and he cried because he did.
C The baby's toy broke, and he cried, because of that.
D The baby cried because he was sad that his toy broke.

Lesson 9
WEEKLY TESTS 9.9

Name _____ Date _____

Storm Warriors
Language Arts

4 What is the **best** way to combine these sentences?

> **I need your help. The zipper on my jacket is stuck.**

A My jacket, I need help, my zipper is stuck.
B Your help on my jacket would help because it is stuck the zipper.
C Help me unzip my jacket, which is now stuck.
D I need your help with the stuck zipper on my jacket.

5 What is the **best** way to combine these sentences?

> **Gabby always wins races. She is a serious runner. She is fast.**

A Gabby always wins races because she is fast.
B Gabby always wins because she is serious and fast.
C Gabby, a serious runner, always wins races because she is fast.
D Gabby wins races only when she is the fastest and the most serious runner.

6 What is the **best** way to combine these sentences?

> **Peter likes vanilla ice cream. May likes vanilla ice cream. They share a pint sometimes.**

A Peter and May like vanilla ice cream, or they share a pint sometimes.
B Sometimes Peter and May like vanilla ice cream and share a pint.
C Since Peter and May both like vanilla ice cream, they sometimes share a pint.
D Peter and May like vanilla ice cream, but Peter and May share a pint sometimes.

Go On

Language Arts
© Houghton Mifflin Harcourt Publishing Company. All rights reserved.

Grade 5, Unit 2: Wild Encounters

Name _____ Date _____

Lesson 9
WEEKLY TESTS 9.10

Storm Warriors
Language Arts

7 What is the **best** way to combine these sentences?

> **Thomas can do handstands. He is very fit. Sometimes he falls.**

A Thomas, very fit, can do handstands and fall sometimes.
B Thomas is very fit, he always falls out of his handstands.
C Thomas, who is very fit, can do handstands, although sometimes he falls.
D Thomas, who is very fit, sometimes does handstands and sometimes Thomas falls.

8 What is the **best** way to combine these sentences?

> **All of the animals at the zoo are interesting. My favorite is one of the elephants. His name is Bozo.**

A Of all the interesting animals at the zoo, I like Bozo the best, so he is an elephant.
B I like all of the animals at the zoo, especially any elephants who are named Bozo.
C Although all the animals at the zoo are interesting, I like the elephant named Bozo the best.
D Of all the interesting animals at the zoo, I only like the elephants and my favorite one is named Bozo.

Language Arts
© Houghton Mifflin Harcourt Publishing Company. All rights reserved.

Grade 5, Unit 2: Wild Encounters

Lesson 9
WEEKLY TESTS 9.11

Storm Warriors
Language Arts

9 What is the **best** way to combine these sentences?

> **The sky was purple and pink. I watched the sunset for a long time.**

A I watched the purple and pink because of the sunset.
B I watched the purple and pink sunset, I watched it for a long time.
C Since the sky was purple and pink, I watched the sunset for a long time.
D When the sky was purple and pink, there was a sunset that I watched for a long time.

10 What is the **best** way to combine these sentences?

> **Your clothing does not match. I think you should change your shirt. Do it quickly before we have to leave.**

A I think your shirt and your pants do not match, so change them.
B I think you should change your shirt quickly before we have to leave.
C I think you should change your shirt quickly, your clothing does not match.
D I think you should change your shirt because your clothing does not match, and do it quickly before we have to leave.

STOP

Language Arts

Grade 5, Unit 2: Wild Encounters

Name _____ Date _____

Lesson 10
WEEKLY TESTS 10.1

Cougars
Test Record Form

TEST RECORD FORM	Possible Score	Criterion Score	Student Score
Vocabulary: Target Vocabulary, Analogies	10	8	
Comprehension: Main Ideas and Details, Selection Test	10	8	
Decoding: Recognizing Schwa + /r/ Sounds	10	8	
Language Arts: Quotations	10	8	
TOTAL	40	32	

Total Student Score × 2.5 = _____ %

Test Record Form
© Houghton Mifflin Harcourt Publishing Company. All rights reserved.

Grade 5, Unit 2: Wild Encounters

Name _____ Date _____

Lesson 10
WEEKLY TESTS 10.2

Target Vocabulary, Analogies

Cougars
Vocabulary

*D*irections
Use what you know about the target vocabulary and analogies to answer questions 1–10. For each question, circle the letter next to your answer choice.

1 What does the word "resemble" mean in the sentence below?

> Those two trees resemble each other.

A look like
B flake off
C grow near
D depend on

2 What does the word "keen" mean in the sentence below?

> The bat has a keen sense of hearing.

A lazy
B sharp
C clever
D awkward

3 What does the word "mature" mean in the sentence below?

> The puppies will grow and mature as they get older.

A sleep more
B gain strength
C develop fully
D become wiser

4 What does the word "particular" mean in the sentence below?

> We drive a particular route to school every day.

A gravel
B bumpy
C certain
D unknown

5 What does the word "ferocious" mean in the sentence below?

> The little kitten tried to act like a ferocious lion.

A savage
B drowsy
C imaginary
D humorous

Go On

Vocabulary
© Houghton Mifflin Harcourt Publishing Company. All rights reserved.

Grade 5, Unit 2: Wild Encounters

Name _____ Date _____

Lesson 10
WEEKLY TESTS 10.3

Cougars
Vocabulary

Directions

Use what you know about analogies to complete the analogies in questions 6–10. For each question, circle the letter next to your answer choice.

6 *Mother* is to *aunt* as *father* is to

A son
B uncle
C nephew
D grandfather

7 *Date* is to *calendar* as *time* is to

A ruler
B scale
C clock
D volume

8 *Break* is to *glass* as *tear* is to

A brick
B paper
C wood
D rubber

9 *Admiral* is to *navy* as *general* is to

A army
B school
C factory
D laboratory

10 *Blue* is to *color* as *circle* is to

A ring
B ball
C shape
D triangle

STOP

Vocabulary
© Houghton Mifflin Harcourt Publishing Company. All rights reserved.

Grade 5, Unit 2: Wild Encounters

Name _____ Date _____

Lesson 10
WEEKLY TESTS 10.4

Cougars
Comprehension

Main Ideas and Details, Selection Test

Directions
Think back to the selection "Cougars" to answer questions 1–10. For each question, circle the letter next to your answer choice.

1 What is the **main** topic of the selection?

A facts about cougars
B where most cougars live
C the cougar's hunting skills
D how cougars raise their young

2 Cougars have very little fat on their bodies and stay warm because they

A have fur coats
B live in warm climates
C are medium-sized cats
D have no sweat glands and pant to release heat

3 Describing cougars' coats and coloring supports the main idea that

A all cougars look the same
B adult cougars look like female lions
C cougars have coats of different colors
D their fur helps keep cougars safe from predators

4 Scientists are unable to tell individual cougars apart because cougars

A vary greatly in color
B are rarely seen by people
C live together in huge groups
D have such good camouflage

5 Which detail supports the main idea that cougars have good eyesight?

A They have a sharp sense of hearing.
B They blend in with their surroundings.
C They have a tawny, or orange-brown, coat.
D They can see moving prey from long distances.

Go On

Comprehension
© Houghton Mifflin Harcourt Publishing Company. All rights reserved.

Grade 5, Unit 2: Wild Encounters

Name _____ Date _____

Lesson 10
WEEKLY TESTS 10.5

Cougars
Comprehension

6 Which of the sentences below states a main idea?

A *Like all of their cat relatives, cougars have whiskers.*
B *These sensitive hairs are also called vibrissae (vy BRIHS ee).*
C *The cougar uses whiskers to gather information through touch.*
D *They grow on either side of the animal's nose and mouth, above the eyes, and sometimes on the chin.*

7 Which detail supports the fact that cougars make a variety of sounds?

A Cougars have a sharp sense of hearing.
B Cougars protect their territory from intruders.
C Cougars hiss and growl when they are threatened.
D Cougars have strong jaws and three kinds of teeth.

8 Cougars groom themselves and their kittens

A to clean their coats
B when they feel threatened
C before they hunt their prey
D so predators can smell the cougars

9 Which detail does not support the main idea that cougars have three kinds of teeth?

A Cougars use canine teeth to puncture prey.
B Cougars use teeth called incisors to cut and chew food.
C Cougars have carnassial teeth on their top and bottom jaws.
D Cougars gulp their food without using their teeth for chewing much.

10 The fact that cougar kittens stay with their mother for about eighteen months supports the idea that

A kittens grow teeth after about two months
B cougar kittens depend on their mothers for food
C young cougars learn to pounce on prey to catch it
D mother cougars groom their kittens like other cats

Mark Student Reading Level:
____ Independent ____ Instructional ____ Listening

STOP

Comprehension
© Houghton Mifflin Harcourt Publishing Company. All rights reserved.

Grade 5, Unit 2: Wild Encounters

Lesson 10
WEEKLY TESTS 10.6

Name _____ Date _____

Cougars
Decoding

Recognizing Schwa + /r/ Sounds

Directions
Use what you know about schwa + /r/ sounds to complete the sentences in questions 1–10. For each question, circle the letter next to your answer choice.

1 What is your favorite _____ of ice cream?

   A flavir
   B flaver
   C flavar
   D flavor

2 Rosie looked at the _____ to see what the date was.

   A calendar
   B calender
   C calendir
   D calendur

3 I have written five _____ of my book.

   A chapters
   B chaptars
   C chaptors
   D chapturs

4 My Uncle Jack is my _____ at school.

   A menter
   B mentor
   C mentore
   D mentawr

5 The newspaper costs one _____.

   A quater
   B quoter
   C quartur
   D quarter

6 What is the _____ way to greet the Queen of England?

   A proper
   B propor
   C propre
   D prowper

Go On

Decoding
Grade 5, Unit 2: Wild Encounters

Name _____ Date _____

Lesson 10
WEEKLY TESTS 10.7

Cougars
Decoding

7 The tourists crossed the _____ at sunrise.

  A boder
  B bordar
  C border
  D bordur

8 Julio was the first _____ on the bus.

  A passenger
  B passengar
  C passengir
  D passengaer

9 Hilda's college _____ tried his best to guide her.

  A advisar
  B adviser
  C advisur
  D advisere

10 It is a wonderful _____ to be here today.

  A honir
  B honer
  C honar
  D honor

STOP

Decoding

Grade 5, Unit 2: Wild Encounters

Name _____ Date _____

Lesson 10
WEEKLY TESTS 10.8

Cougars
Language Arts

Quotations

*D*irections
Use what you know about quotations to answer questions 1–10. For each question, circle the letter next to your answer choice.

1 Which sentence is written correctly?

  A Tony said, "I will trim the trees tomorrow morning."
  B "Tony said, I will trim the trees tomorrow morning."
  C Tony "said, I will trim the trees tomorrow morning."
  D "Tony said, "I will trim the trees tomorrow morning.

2 Which sentence is written correctly?

  A "Do you know what time the train will arrive" asked Marty?
  B Do you know what time the train will arrive? "asked Marty."
  C "Do you know what time" the train will arrive asked Marty?
  D "Do you know what time the train will arrive?" asked Marty.

3 Which sentence is written correctly?

  A "Our math test is on Friday, stated Tyler."
  B "Our math test is on Friday," stated Tyler.
  C "Our math test is on Friday" stated Tyler.
  D Our math test is on Friday. "stated Tyler."

4 Which sentence is written correctly?

  A Grandpa bakes the best apple pie in the world! "exclaimed Suki."
  B Grandpa, "Bakes the best apple pie in the world" exclaimed Suki!
  C "Grandpa bakes the best apple pie in the world!" exclaimed Suki.
  D "Grandpa bakes the best apple pie in the world exclaimed Suki!"

Go On

Language Arts
© Houghton Mifflin Harcourt Publishing Company. All rights reserved.

Grade 5, Unit 2: Wild Encounters

Lesson 10
WEEKLY TESTS 10.9

Name _____ Date _____

Cougars
Language Arts

5 Which sentence is written correctly?

　A Joey laughed, "Look at those cute puppies." They are playing with a toy.
　B Joey laughed, Look at those cute puppies. "They are playing with a toy."
　C Joey laughed, "Look at those cute puppies. They are playing with a toy."
　D "Joey laughed. Look at those cute puppies. They are playing with a toy."

6 Which sentence is written correctly?

　A Lee remarked, "Rosa and Rita are twins who look exactly alike."
　B Lee remarked Rosa and Rita, "are twins who look exactly alike."
　C Lee remarked "Rosa and Rita are twins who look exactly alike."
　D "Lee remarked Rosa and Rita are twins who look exactly alike."

7 Which sentence is written correctly?

　A "Renee complained, I don't want to go because I have a headache."
　B "Renee complained." I don't want to go because I have a headache.
　C Renee complained "I don't want to go because I have a headache.
　D Renee complained, "I don't want to go because I have a headache."

8 Which sentence is written correctly?

　A "We can go to the library after the baby takes a nap. Mom said."
　B We can go to the library after the baby takes a nap, "Mom said."
　C "We can go to the library after the baby takes a nap," Mom said.
　D "We can go to the library," After the baby takes a nap Mom said.

Language Arts
© Houghton Mifflin Harcourt Publishing Company. All rights reserved.

Grade 5, Unit 2: Wild Encounters

Name _____ Date _____

Lesson 10
WEEKLY TESTS 10.10

Cougars
Language Arts

9 Which sentence is written correctly?

   A Lisa asked, "Sue, did you have fun at the picnic?"
   B Lisa asked? Sue, "Did you have fun at the picnic."
   C "Lisa asked? Sue did you have fun at the picnic?"
   D Lisa asked, "Sue," did you have fun at the picnic?

10 Which sentence is written correctly?

   A "Do you know a store that sells kites, model cars, and board games? Steve inquired."
   B "Do you know a store that sells kites, model cars, and board games?" Steve inquired.
   C Do you know a store that sells kites, model cars, and board games? "Steve inquired."
   D "Do you know a store that sells kites, model cars, and board games," Steve inquired?

STOP

Language Arts

Grade 5, Unit 2: Wild Encounters

Name _____ Date _____

Lesson 11
WEEKLY TESTS 11.1

Dangerous Crossingh
Test Record Form

TEST RECORD FORM	Possible Score	Criterion Score	Student Score
Vocabulary: Target Vocabulary, Using Reference Sources	10	8	
Comprehension: Cause and Effect, Selection Test	10	8	
Decoding: Vowel Sounds in Stressed Syllables	10	8	
Language Arts: Subject and Object Pronouns	10	8	
TOTAL	40	32	
		Total Student Score × 2.5 =	%

Test Record Form
© Houghton Mifflin Harcourt Publishing Company. All rights reserved.

Grade 5, Unit 3: Revolution!

Name _____ Date _____

Target Vocabulary, Using Reference Sources

Lesson 11
WEEKLY TESTS 11.2

Dangerous Crossing
Vocabulary

Directions
Use what you know about the target vocabulary and using reference sources to answer questions 1–10. For each question, circle the letter next to your answer choice.

1 What does the word "representatives" mean in the sentence below?

> There were representatives from each state at the conference.

A people who serve as agents
B items that are used as money
C documents that are important
D minerals that are in the ground

2 What does the word "cramped" mean in the sentence below?

> There were so many boxes that the garage felt cramped.

A tired
B delicate
C irrigated
D crowded

3 What does the word "distracted" mean in the sentence below?

> The boy could not study because he was distracted by the noise in the library.

A not interested in
B had pledged an oath
C had looked for the source
D had his attention drawn away

4 What does the word "viewpoint" mean in the sentence below?

> The scientist had a good viewpoint to observe the eagle's nest.

A a time that happened many years ago
B a place where something can easily be seen
C a problem that has many different solutions
D a person who takes a lot of time to complete a job

Go On

Vocabulary
© Houghton Mifflin Harcourt Publishing Company. All rights reserved.

Grade 5, Unit 3: Revolution!

Name _____ Date _____

Lesson 11
WEEKLY TESTS 11.3

Dangerous Crossing
Vocabulary

5 What does the word "shattered" mean in the sentence below?

> **The vase shattered when it hit the ground.**

A broke
B drove
C sparkled
D reflected

6 Read the dictionary entry below for the word "broad."

> **broad** \brawd\ *adjective*
> **1.** very wide **2.** full **3.** general
> **4.** free

Which definition represents the meaning of "broad" as it is used in the sentence below?

> **The students wrote a broad outline to use when studying for their test.**

A Definition 1
B Definition 2
C Definition 3
D Definition 4

7 Read the dictionary entry below for the word "hurdle."

> **hurdle** \hur-dl\ *verb* **1.** to jump over **2.** to be successful with solving a problem *noun* **3.** something a runner must jump over **4.** a difficult problem

Which definition represents the meaning of "hurdle" as it is used in the sentence below?

> **The biggest hurdle Naomi faced was learning to feel comfortable in front of an audience.**

A Definition 1
B Definition 2
C Definition 3
D Definition 4

Vocabulary

Grade 5, Unit 3: Revolution!

Name _____ Date _____

Lesson 11
WEEKLY TESTS 11.4

Dangerous Crossing
Vocabulary

8 Read the thesaurus entry below for the word "erase."

> **erase** *verb*: cancel, kill, root, rub

Which word from the entry could be used in place of the word "erase" as it is used in the sentence below?

> **Jacob had to erase the order for a new bike.**

A rub
B kill
C root
D cancel

9 Read the thesaurus entry below for the word "trace."

> **trace** *verb*: copy, map, show, track

Which word from the entry could be used in place of the word "trace" as it is used in the sentence below?

> **Joanne likes to trace pictures on her notebook.**

A map
B copy
C show
D track

10 Read the glossary entries below.

> **aviator** a person who flies an airplane
> **dentist** a person who is trained to care for teeth and gums
> **professor** a person who is a teacher in a college or university
> **secretary** a person who is in charge of records and other company business

Which word from the glossary refers to a person who teaches others?

A dentist
B aviator
C professor
D secretary

STOP

Vocabulary

Grade 5, Unit 3: Revolution!

Name _____ Date _____

Lesson 11
WEEKLY TESTS 11.5

Cause and Effect, Selection Test

Dangerous Crossing
Comprehension

Directions
Think back to the selection "Dangerous Crossing" to answer questions 1–10. For each question, circle the letter next to your answer choice.

1 What effect were the new Americans hoping for by sending John Adams to France?

- **A** for Adams to get out of the war zone
- **B** for Adams's son to get out of the war zone
- **C** for Adams to convince England to surrender to the Americans
- **D** for Adams to convince France to help the Americans

2 What is the **most likely** reason John Adams and his son traveled by barge to the ship?

- **A** The ship had been damaged by the storm and needed to be repaired.
- **B** The passengers were sneaking onto the ship because they could not afford tickets.
- **C** The ship was so large it would have gotten stuck if it had come close to the shore.
- **D** The passengers were hoping the weather would improve by the time they got to the ship.

3 What was the cause of Johnny's illness?

- **A** He was seasick.
- **B** He was sick with a virus.
- **C** He was afraid of enemy boats.
- **D** He was afraid of the long journey.

4 What caused Johnny and his father to feel better on the second day of their journey?

- **A** the rain
- **B** the calmer sea
- **C** the end of the war
- **D** the retreat of the frigate

5 After Johnny and his father retreated to their cabin, what caused the ship to pitch?

- **A** a storm
- **B** a cannon fired by the British
- **C** a problem with the ship
- **D** a British troop boarding the ship

Comprehension
© Houghton Mifflin Harcourt Publishing Company. All rights reserved.

Grade 5, Unit 3: Revolution!

Name _____ Date _____

Lesson 11
WEEKLY TESTS 11.6

Dangerous Crossing
Comprehension

6 What did Johnny and his father assume was the cause of the flash of light?

- **A** the storm
- **B** enemy fire
- **C** the ship got off course
- **D** a malfunction in the ship

7 What caused four crew members to get hurt?

- **A** The ship was hit by lightning.
- **B** The ship was hit by enemy fire.
- **C** The ship was steered off course.
- **D** The ship was hit by an enemy ship.

8 Johnny had time to take French lessons because he was waiting for the

- **A** storm to end
- **B** war to be over
- **C** barge to arrive
- **D** ship to be repaired

9 Why did the sailor keep Johnny away from the man-of-war?

- **A** He did not want the boy to get stung.
- **B** He did not want the boy to get killed.
- **C** He did not want the boy to hurt the man-of-war.
- **D** He did not want the boy to eat the crew's dinner.

10 Why was Captain Tucker angry about John Adams coming on deck when the *Boston* was attacked by a British merchantman?

- **A** He did not have a weapon for John.
- **B** He did not want John to get injured.
- **C** He did not like having John as a passenger.
- **D** He did not want John to get in the crew's way.

Mark Student Reading Level:

____ Independent ____ Instructional ____ Listening

STOP

Comprehension

Name _____ Date _____

Vowel Sounds in Stressed Syllables

Lesson 11
WEEKLY TESTS 11.7

Dangerous Crossing
Decoding

*D*irections
Use what you know about vowel sounds in stressed syllables to answer questions 1–10. For each question, circle the letter next to your answer choice.

1. I love shopping for a _____ at the store.
   A bergain
   B bargain
   C bairgain
   D bahrgain

2. That material has an interesting _____.
   A pattern
   B puttern
   C paittern
   D paettern

3. Jacob hurt his _____ during the football game.
   A shulder
   B sholder
   C shoulder
   D shoelder

4. If you got lost in the _____, would you know how to survive?
   A farest
   B forest
   C fahrest
   D foerest

5. Sheila said, "Perhaps I will go to the _____ after all."
   A party
   B porty
   C pahrty
   D pawty

6. Ira will _____ to walk on the balance beam.
   A attempt
   B attumpt
   C attiempt
   D atteampt

Decoding
© Houghton Mifflin Harcourt Publishing Company. All rights reserved.

Grade 5, Unit 3: Revolution!

Lesson 11
WEEKLY TESTS 11.8

Name _____ Date _____

Dangerous Crossing
Decoding

7 The _____ on the train seemed to take forever.

- A jerney
- B jurney
- C joerney
- D journey

8 The _____ argued her case in front of the judge.

- A lawyer
- B lowyer
- C loiwyer
- D louwyer

9 My older brother is also my _____.

- A mintor
- B mentor
- C meintor
- D meantor

10 The ship did not _____ with the iceberg.

- A collide
- B collyde
- C colliede
- D collayde

STOP

Name _____ Date _____

Lesson 11
WEEKLY TESTS 11.9

Subject and Object Pronouns

Dangerous Crossing
Language Arts

*D*irections
Use what you know about subject and object pronouns to answer questions 1–10. For each question, circle the letter next to your answer choice.

1 Which sentence is written correctly?

   A He tells we to pack our belongings.
   B Us are excited about moving to a new place.
   C My father watches us move about in our new home.
   D Him dreams of living in a bigger house in California.

2 Which sentence is written correctly?

   A Mrs. Jackson teaches I and my classmates.
   B Them are not easy to teach a new language.
   C Her is a woman who has taught for many years.
   D She is in charge of students during school field trips.

3 Which sentence is written correctly?

   A Maybe a wild animal scared them.
   B Them are galloping around the corral.
   C Ben and me think something startled the horses.
   D I and you should go see what is wrong with they.

4 Which sentence is written correctly?

   A The rabbits will hop to her.
   B Them will like the fresh carrots.
   C Her always knows how to care for rabbits.
   D Me see that Mary brought carrots for the rabbits.

Language Arts
© Houghton Mifflin Harcourt Publishing Company. All rights reserved.

Grade 5, Unit 3: Revolution!

Name _____ Date _____

Lesson 11
WEEKLY TESTS 11.10

Dangerous Crossing
Language Arts

5 Which sentence is written correctly?

A That fence will keep they safe.
B We saw fish swimming in the pond.
C Ben and me watched the cattle in the pasture.
D Us will have to feed the chickens in the morning.

6 Which sentence is written correctly?

A The cat jumped out of him bed.
B The cat will eat when he is hungry.
C Martin and me heard us cat purring.
D I will feed they this new type of cat food.

7 Which sentence is written correctly?

A She mother went to see her doctor.
B The doctor gave she some medicine.
C Me and Darby hope her feels better soon.
D She did not come because Suzy's mother is sick.

8 Which sentence is written correctly?

A Her lives in Idaho near me cousins.
B She will go with I to visit Grandma.
C Aunt Polly and me like to play games.
D Aunt Polly was on the airplane with me.

9 Which sentence is written correctly?

A Her will think we are concerned citizens.
B Us hope the mayor will have the light fixed.
C Me and Orli are going to write a letter to the mayor.
D Orli cannot sleep with street lights shining in her eyes.

10 Which sentence is written correctly?

A Jake's band will play for us class.
B Him learned to play the guitar last year.
C I will give Jake some of me music to play.
D Jake's band is so loud that his father complains.

STOP

Language Arts
© Houghton Mifflin Harcourt Publishing Company. All rights reserved.

Grade 5, Unit 3: Revolution!

Name _____ Date _____

Lesson 12
WEEKLY TESTS 12.1

Can't You Make Them Behave, King George?
Test Record Form

TEST RECORD FORM	Possible Score	Criterion Score	Student Score
Vocabulary: Target Vocabulary, Using Context	10	8	
Comprehension: Fact and Opinion, Selection Test	10	8	
Decoding: Open and Closed Syllables: VCV Pattern	10	8	
Language Arts: Verb Tenses	10	8	
TOTAL	40	32	
		Total Student Score × 2.5 =	%

Test Record Form
© Houghton Mifflin Harcourt Publishing Company. All rights reserved.

Grade 5, Unit 3: Revolution!

Name _____ Date _____

Lesson 12
WEEKLY TESTS 12.2

Target Vocabulary, Using Context

Can't You Make Them Behave, King George?
Vocabulary

*D*irections
Use what you know about the target vocabulary and using context to answer questions 1–10. For each question, circle the letter next to your answer choice.

1 What does the word "objected" mean in the sentence below?

> **Neal objected to painting the house yellow.**

A opposed
B reflected
C discussed
D challenged

2 What does the word "midst" mean in the sentence below?

> **The famous actor stood unnoticed in the midst of the crowd.**

A next to
B ahead of
C apart from
D surrounded by

3 What does the word "advantages" mean in the sentence below?

> **There are many advantages to having a recycling program.**

A benefits
B solutions
C instructions
D celebrations

4 What does the word "temporary" mean in the sentence below?

> **The dentist put a temporary filling in David's tooth.**

A having a good flavor
B lasting only a short time
C using invisible materials
D costing very little money

Go On

Vocabulary
© Houghton Mifflin Harcourt Publishing Company. All rights reserved.

Grade 5, Unit 3: Revolution!

Lesson 12
WEEKLY TESTS 12.3

Name _____ Date _____

Can't You Make Them Behave, King George?
Vocabulary

5 What does the word "repeal" mean in the sentence below?

The voters decided to repeal the unfair law.

A forge
B cancel
C disguise
D appreciate

6 What does the word "cautious" mean in the sentence below?

It is important to be cautious when crossing the street.

A careful
B clumsy
C confident
D conscious

7 What does the word "device" mean in the sentence below?

The scientist built a device to pick up trash.

A part of a plan
B section of land
C type of garment
D piece of equipment

8 What does the word "merchant" mean in the sentence below?

The merchant sold his goods at the market.

A trader
B peasant
C descendant
D bookkeeper

9 What does the word "patrol" mean in the sentence below?

The new police officer will patrol the park.

A clean
B guard
C include
D describe

10 What does the word "ridiculous" mean in the sentence below?

Alvin thought he looked ridiculous in the chipmunk costume.

A silly
B cold
C invisible
D handsome

STOP

Vocabulary
© Houghton Mifflin Harcourt Publishing Company. All rights reserved.

Grade 5, Unit 3: Revolution!

Lesson 12
WEEKLY TESTS 12.4

Name _____ Date _____

Can't You Make Them Behave, King George?
Comprehension

Fact and Opinion, Selection Test

Directions

Think back to the selection "Can't You Make Them Behave, King George?" to answer questions 1–10. For each question, circle the letter next to your answer choice.

1 Which of these statements is a **fact**?

  A Taxing Americans was a good idea.
  B England had the right to tax the colonies.
  C The French and Indian War was fought in America.
  D When George came to the throne, England had been fighting a long and expensive war.

2 Whose **opinion** is expressed in this quote?

  "After all, the French and Indian part of the war had been fought on American soil for the benefit of Americans, so why shouldn't they help pay for it?"

  A the author's
  B the king's
  C the colonists'
  D the English soldiers'

3 Which word indicates that this statement is an **opinion**?

  "King George believed that above all a king should be firm...."

  A *King*
  B *believed*
  C *above*
  D *firm*

4 Which of these sentences from the selection is an **opinion**?

  A The English troops captured New York.
  B For a while, King George had every reason to feel confident.
  C Instead, on July 4, 1776, Americans declared their independence.
  D When the tea arrived in Boston, they dumped it into the Boston Harbor.

Go On

Comprehension
© Houghton Mifflin Harcourt Publishing Company. All rights reserved.

Grade 5, Unit 3: Revolution!

Name _____ Date _____

Lesson 12
WEEKLY TESTS 12.5

Can't You Make Them Behave, King George?
Comprehension

5 Which word indicates that this statement is an **opinion**?

> "He was, for instance, the most prayed-for man in the empire."

A *was*
B *most*
C *empire*
D *instance*

6 Which word in this statement expresses an **opinion**?

> "France, impressed with the victory at Saratoga, joined the war on America's side."

A *side*
B *joined*
C *victory*
D *impressed*

7 Which of these sentences from the selection is a **fact**?

A *Good kings deserve to win.*
B *All he had to do was to show the world that he wasn't the least bit worried.*
C *For the last 10 years of his life he was a wretched-looking figure dressed in a purple bathrobe with wide white hair and wild beard.*
D *He died in 1820 at the age of 82.*

8 What was Lord North's **opinion** when he heard about the events at Yorktown?

A King George would be overthrown.
B The war would last a very long time.
C The colonists were going to win the war.
D England needed the next battle to be a victory.

Comprehension
© Houghton Mifflin Harcourt Publishing Company. All rights reserved.

Grade 5, Unit 3: Revolution!

Name _____ Date _____

Lesson 12
WEEKLY TESTS 12.6

Can't You Make Them Behave, King George?
Comprehension

9 Which of these sentences from the selection is a **fact**?

   A *King George couldn't fight the war all by himself.*
   B *So when the time came for him to sign the peace proclamation, he signed.*
   C *As long as he lived, King George had nightmares about the loss of the American colonies.*
   D *It certainly hadn't been his fault, he said.*

10 Which **fact** would best support the **opinion** that King George's taxes were not a good idea?

   A The Americans were English subjects.
   B The English government needed money.
   C The taxes led to the loss of the American colonies.
   D The French and Indian War benefited the Americans.

Mark Student Reading Level:
____ Independent ____ Instructional ____ Listening

STOP

Comprehension
© Houghton Mifflin Harcourt Publishing Company. All rights reserved.

Grade 5, Unit 3: Revolution!

Lesson 12
WEEKLY TESTS 12.7

Name _____ Date _____

Can't You Make Them Behave, King George?
Decoding

Open and Closed Syllables: VCV Pattern

Directions
Use what you know about open and closed syllables to choose the correct way to divide the underlined words in sentences 1–10. For each question, circle the letter next to your answer choice.

1 Patty had a vivid dream last night.
  A vi • vid
  B viv • id
  C vivi • d
  D v • ivid

2 I love looking at modern art.
  A mode • rn
  B mo • dern
  C mod • ern
  D mo • de • rn

3 Uta will select the finest vegetables from the market.
  A sel • ect
  B sele • ct
  C s • elect
  D se • lect

4 Nancy's favorite season is autumn.
  A aut • umn
  B autu • mn
  C au • tumn
  D au • tu • mn

5 The magician's tricks will amaze you.
  A a • maze
  B am • aze
  C ama • ze
  D amaz • e

6 Sarita studied the menu.
  A m • en • u
  B m • enu
  C men • u
  D me • nu

7 Robert said, "I don't deserve this award!"
  A des • erve
  B de • serve
  C dese • rve
  D deser • ve

8 The construction noise was becoming a nuisance.
  A nu • isance
  B nui • sance
  C nuis • ance
  D nuisan • ce

Decoding

Grade 5, Unit 3: Revolution!

Name _____ Date _____

Lesson 12
WEEKLY TESTS 12.8

Can't You Make Them Behave, King George?
Decoding

9 Tito is my first <u>cousin</u>.

A co • usin
B cou • sin
C cous • in
D c • ous • in

10 Which <u>item</u> would Luke like to buy?

A i • tem
B it • em
C ite • m
D i • te • m

STOP

Decoding

Grade 5, Unit 3: Revolution!

Name _____   Date _____

Verb Tenses

Lesson 12
WEEKLY TESTS 12.9

Can't You Make Them Behave, King George?
Language Arts

*D*irections
Use what you know about verb tenses to answer questions 1–10. For each question, circle the letter next to your answer choice.

1 Which sentence is written correctly?

  A Next week I rented two pairs of ice skates.
  B Last month my sister and I will learn a new sport.
  C Yesterday, my sister and I nervously glide onto the ice.
  D We watched our friends at the skating rink two weeks ago.

2 Which sentence is written correctly?

  A Last year I like to ride my bike to school.
  B Next week, my friend Juan rode with me.
  C We will park our bikes outside our school's entrance.
  D Last week, we will plan to hurry home to play baseball.

3 Which sentence is written correctly?

  A Many teams from our school will attend.
  B We hope to win the championship last year.
  C Our school sponsored a soccer tournament next week.
  D Next week, our school team hoped to win the championship.

4 Which sentence is written correctly?

  A He will attend his new school yesterday.
  B He enjoys meeting his classmates earlier.
  C Mario moves into his new house last weekend.
  D He thinks he will like his new home and school.

Language Arts
© Houghton Mifflin Harcourt Publishing Company. All rights reserved.

Grade 5, Unit 3: Revolution!

Lesson 12
WEEKLY TESTS 12.10

Name _____ Date _____

Can't You Make Them Behave, King George?
Language Arts

5 Which sentence is written correctly?

A They flew the kite tomorrow.
B Many of their friends will made kites, too.
C Tomorrow the sky will be filled with kites.
D The boys will make a big yellow kite yesterday.

6 Which sentence is written correctly?

A I have eaten her cake next week.
B Mom will bake a cake last week.
C I love to eat Mom's chocolate cake.
D The chocolate cake is eaten yesterday.

7 Which sentence is written correctly?

A Will you go to yesterday's meeting?
B Did you enjoy the meeting next August?
C Cindy does not like to go to the meetings.
D Ted and Cindy will go to the meetings last year.

8 Which sentence is written correctly?

A After we ate the turkey, I will serve the pumpkin pie.
B I always look forward to eating Thanksgiving dinner.
C Juan and Miriam ate all of the turkey tomorrow morning!
D Please cooked a turkey for next year's Thanksgiving meal.

9 Which sentence is written correctly?

A I have done tomorrow's homework.
B I will do my homework yesterday afternoon.
C I have done all of my homework tomorrow afternoon.
D Why do we already have gotten homework for next week?

10 Which sentence is written correctly?

A Let's have played jump rope later.
B Get the jump rope for me yesterday.
C I love jumping rope every Thursday.
D I tripped on the jump rope next week.

STOP

Language Arts
© Houghton Mifflin Harcourt Publishing Company. All rights reserved.

Grade 5, Unit 3: Revolution!

Name _____ Date _____

Lesson 13
WEEKLY TESTS 13.1

They Called Her Molly Pitcher
Test Record Form

TEST RECORD FORM	Possible Score	Criterion Score	Student Score
Skills in Context: Conclusions and Generalizations, Target Vocabulary	10	8	
Vocabulary: Target Vocabulary, Use a Thesaurus	10	8	
Comprehension: Conclusions and Generalizations, Selection Test	10	8	
Decoding: Recognizing Initial and Medial Digraphs	10	8	
Language Arts: Regular and Irregular Verbs	10	8	
TOTAL	50	42	
		Total Student Score × 2 =	%

Test Record Form
© Houghton Mifflin Harcourt Publishing Company. All rights reserved.

Grade 5, Unit 3: Revolution!

Name _____ Date _____

Lesson 13
WEEKLY TESTS 13.2

Conclusions and Generalizations, Target Vocabulary

They Called Her Molly Pitcher
Skills in Context

Directions
Read each selection. Then read each question that follows the selections. Decide which is the best answer to each question. For each question, circle the letter next to your answer choice.

Linda Brown

In the early 1950s, Linda Brown of Topeka, Kansas, wanted to go to school with other children in her neighborhood. Instead, she had to walk one mile, through a railroad yard, to a bus stop where she would begin a two-mile ride to a different school.

Why did Linda have to travel so far to go to school? Because she was African American, and at that time, elementary schools in some states were segregated. Linda Brown's family and twelve other African American families decided to fight against the laws that upheld segregation in the schools. The families went to the all-white schools near their homes and tried to enroll their children.

Linda Brown said later ". . . well, like I say, we lived in an integrated neighborhood, and I had all of these playmates of different nationalities.

And so when I found out that day that I might be able to go to their school, I was just thrilled, you know.

"And I remember walking over to Sumner school with my dad that day and going up the steps of the school, and the school looked so big to a smaller child. And I remember going inside, and my dad spoke with someone, and then he went into the inner office with the principal, and they left me out . . . to sit outside with the secretary.

"And while he was in the inner office, I could hear voices and hear his voice raised, you know, as the conversation went on. And then he immediately came out of the office, took me by the hand, and we walked home from the school. I just couldn't understand what was happening because I was so sure that I was going to go to school with . . . all of my playmates."

Go On

When the families were turned away and sent to the all-black schools, a lawsuit was filed. In 1951, an organization called the National Association for the Advancement of Colored People (NAACP) agreed to help. One of its lawyers, Thurgood Marshall, presented the case before the Supreme Court. The case became known as *Brown v. Board of Education of Topeka*. Marshall argued that separate schools did not provide an equal education.

In 1954, all nine justices of the Supreme Court ruled the same way. They decided that providing separate educational experiences for white and African American children was against the law. They believed that children who were treated differently would not achieve as much in school. A new revolution had begun — that of equality in education.

The case was a giant step toward equal education for all children. However, the court did not set a definite time for all schools to be desegregated. It took many more years and many more court battles for America to finally enjoy fully integrated schools.

The Little Rock Nine

The Fourteenth Amendment to the Constitution of the United States says that everyone is equal under the laws of our country. Still, people were segregated or separated by race. Many communities had what became known as "separeate but equal" policies. For example, African American students could not go to the same schools as white students.

Many people did not want people of a different race to use the same things they used. They fought against integration. In some places, schools were closed so that African American students could not attend them. Sometimes, the federal government stepped in to make sure that people were treated equally.

Lesson 13
WEEKLY TESTS 13.4

Name _____ Date _____

They Called Her Molly Pitcher
Skills in Context

In 1957, nine African American students tried to enter Central High School in Little Rock, Arkansas. The state's governor sent the Arkansas National Guard to stop them, but the students knew they could not retreat. The President sent federal soldiers to escort the students into the school and to protect their right to attend the school.

These students became known as the Little Rock Nine. They helped lead the way for the integration of public schools in Little Rock. In May 1958, Ernest Green became the first African American to graduate from Central High. Today, the school is a national historic site and serves as a reminder of the struggle for equality that happened there.

Use the selection "Linda Brown" to answer questions 1–4. For each question, circle the letter next to your answer choice.

1 Linda Brown was surprised that she had to go to a school far from her home because she

  A lived in an integrated neighborhood
  B had attended the same school her whole life
  C had older brothers and sisters who had gone to the nearby school
  D lived near other African Americans who went to the neighborhood school

2 What generalization can be made about the Supreme Court justices in the 1950s?

  A They cared about children.
  B They supported segregation.
  C They believed that white teachers should be paid higher wages.
  D They thought schools did a poor job of educating students.

Go On

Lesson 13
WEEKLY TESTS 13.5

They Called Her Molly Pitcher
Skills in Context

Name _____ Date _____

3 What does the word "revolution" mean as used in the passage?

    A war
    B rule
    C change
    D integration

4 According to the selection, which event occurred in 1951?

    A *All nine justices of the Supreme Court ruled the same way.*
    B *Families went to the all-white schools near their homes and tried to enroll their children.*
    C *An organization called the National Association for the Advancement of Colored People (NAACP) agreed to help.*
    D *Linda Brown's family and twelve other African American families decided to fight against the laws that upheld segregation in the schools.*

Name _____ Date _____

Lesson 13
WEEKLY TESTS 13.6

They Called Her Molly Pitcher
Skills in Context

Use the selection "The Little Rock Nine" to answer questions 5–8. For each question, circle the letter next to your answer choice.

5 Which amendment says that all people are equal in the United States?

A The Ninth Amendment
B The Twelfth Amendment
C The Thirteenth Amendment
D The Fourteenth Amendment

6 Why did some schools in Little Rock close?

A to save the school districts money
B to keep white students out of the schools
C to allow time for the schools to be repaired
D to keep African American students out of the schools

7 What does the word "retreat" mean as used in the passage?

A relax
B escape
C triumph
D withdraw

8 Using the events in Little Rock in 1957, what conclusion can you draw about the President?

A He supported integrating the country's schools.
B He trusted the local police to protect the students.
C He thought students could get a separate but equal education.
D He believed African Americans should be kept segregated.

Go On

Lesson 13
WEEKLY TESTS 13.7

Name _____ Date _____

They Called Her Molly Pitcher
Skills in Context

Use the selections "Linda Brown" and "The Little Rock Nine" to answer questions 9 and 10. For each question, circle the letter next to your answer choice.

9 Why did the author write these two selections?

  A to show how people affected important events in history
  B to persuade people to always respect the rights of others
  C to teach a lesson about the people who wrote the Constitution
  D to entertain with stories about the African American culture

10 How were the events in Topeka similar to the events in Little Rock?

  A African Americans were forced to walk to school.
  B African Americans got protection from federal soldiers.
  C African Americans protested by marching down city streets.
  D African Americans fought against segregation in the schools.

STOP

Lesson 13
WEEKLY TESTS 13.8

Name _____ Date _____

They Called Her Molly Pitcher
Vocabulary

Target Vocabulary, Use a Thesaurus

Directions
Use what you know about the target vocabulary and using a thesaurus to answer questions 1–10. For each question, circle the letter next to your answer choice.

1 What does the word "strategy" mean in the sentence below?

> Daniel chose a strategy for solving the math problem.

A time to work
B book to study
C plan of action
D tool for writing

2 What does the word "magnificent" mean in the sentence below?

> The Grand Canyon is a magnificent sight.

A boring
B rugged
C splendid
D miserable

3 What does the word "foes" mean in the sentence below?

> The two soldiers, who had once been foes, soon became good friends.

A enemies
B peasants
C lawyers
D apprentices

4 What does the word "shimmering" mean in the sentence below?

> The stars were shimmering in the night sky.

A blooming
B glimmering
C condensing
D multiplying

Go On

Vocabulary
© Houghton Mifflin Harcourt Publishing Company. All rights reserved.

Grade 5, Unit 3: Revolution!

Name _____ Date _____

Lesson 13
WEEKLY TESTS 13.9

They Called Her Molly Pitcher
Vocabulary

5 What does the word "gushed" mean in the sentence below?

> **The water gushed from the fountain.**

A trickled slowly
B dripped one drop at a time
C ran dry after a short time
D flowed forth in a great amount

6 Read the thesaurus entry below for the word "adapt."

> **adapt** *verb*: arrange, change, fit, shape

Which word from the entry could be used in place of the word "adapt" as it is used in the following sentence?

> **The lizard is able to adapt to live in different environments.**

A fit
B shape
C change
D arrange

7 Read the thesaurus entry below for the word "channel."

> **channel** *noun*: agent, canal, instrument, route

Which word from the entry could be used in place of the word "channel" as it is used in the following sentence?

> **The boat floated on the water in the channel.**

A agent
B route
C canal
D instrument

8 Read the thesaurus entry below for the word "purse."

> **purse** *noun*: frame, prize, sack, wallet

Which word from the entry could be used in place of the word "purse" as it is used in the following sentence?

> **The purse for winning the race was a gold coin.**

A sack
B prize
C frame
D wallet

Vocabulary
© Houghton Mifflin Harcourt Publishing Company. All rights reserved.

Grade 5, Unit 3: Revolution!

Name _____ Date _____

Lesson 13
WEEKLY TESTS 13.10

They Called Her Molly Pitcher
Vocabulary

9 Read the thesaurus entry below for the word "section."

> **section** *noun*: area, piece, sample, zone

Which word from the entry could be used in place of the word "section" as it is used in the following sentence?

I want a large section of pecan pie, please.

A area
B zone
C piece
D sample

10 Read the thesaurus entry below for the word "grant."

> **grant** *verb*: admit, drop, give, own

Which word from the entry could be used in place of the word "grant" as it is used in the following sentence?

The teacher will grant her students permission to go to the library.

A own
B give
C drop
D admit

STOP

Vocabulary

Grade 5, Unit 3: Revolution!

Lesson 13
WEEKLY TESTS 13.11

Name _____ Date _____

Conclusions and Generalizations, Selection Test

They Called Her Molly Pitcher
Comprehension

*D*irections
Think back to the selection "They Called Her Molly Pitcher" to answer questions 1–10. For each question, circle the letter next to your answer choice.

1 After reading the first two paragraphs of the selection, you can draw all of the following conclusions except that the troops

  A were hungry
  B needed more supplies
  C included both men and women
  D were cold because of the snow

2 What was the basis for the following conclusion?

  "The fight everyone had been preparing for was coming very soon."

  A A scout brought news at the end of June.
  B William Hays was part of Lee's advance guard.
  C General Washington ordered General Lee to lead an advance guard.
  D A large number of British soldiers were gathered at Monmouth Courthouse.

3 What conclusion can the reader draw from this sentence?

  "Winter at Valley Forge had been bitter cold, but June of 1778 in New Jersey was hotter than anyone could remember."

  A The author prefers summer to winter.
  B The author prefers winter to summer.
  C The author skips several months in the narrative.
  D The author flashes back to an earlier point in the narrative.

4 What generalizations can you make about Molly Pitcher?

  A She was brave and caring.
  B She was jealous and mean.
  C She was strong and powerful.
  D She was fearful and awkward.

Comprehension
© Houghton Mifflin Harcourt Publishing Company. All rights reserved.

Grade 5, Unit 3: Revolution!

Name _____ **Date** _____

Lesson 13
WEEKLY TESTS 13.12

They Called Her Molly Pitcher
Comprehension

5 Which sentence supports the conclusion that Molly risked her life when she brought the troops water?

A *Molly paid no attention.*
B *The Americans knew all about such hot and humid days.*
C *She'd spotted a green and mossy place where a spring gushed up.*
D *She raced back to the battlefield, dodging cannon and musket fire, carrying her pitcher of water for any American soldier who needed a drink.*

6 What conclusion can you draw about how the troops felt about Molly on the day that she brought them water?

A They were angry.
B They were curious.
C They were grateful.
D They were confused.

7 What caused the death of fifty-six British soldiers during the battle?

A cannon fire
B heat stroke
C musket fire
D lack of water

8 What conclusion can you draw from General Washington's surprise when he saw Molly firing the cannon?

A He had thought that Molly was a coward.
B He had thought that Molly belonged at home.
C It was very unusual for women to fire cannons.
D It was against army rules for women to fire cannons.

9 What conclusion can you draw about the rank of sergeant in the army?

A It was reserved for men.
B It was reserved for women.
C It was a high honor and unusual for a woman to earn.
D It was only awarded to people who brought water to the troops.

10 Why did the British retreat after the first day of battle?

A They ran out of soldiers.
B The ran out of ammunition.
C They were afraid they would lose.
D They were afraid of Molly Pitcher.

Mark Student Reading Level:
____ Independent ____ Instructional ____ Listening

STOP

Comprehension
© Houghton Mifflin Harcourt Publishing Company. All rights reserved.

Grade 5, Unit 3: Revolution!

Name _____ Date _____

Recognizing Initial and Medial Digraphs

Lesson 13
WEEKLY TESTS 13.13

They Called Her Molly Pitcher
Decoding

*D*irections
Use what you know about initial and medial digraphs to complete sentences 1–10. For each question, circle the letter next to your answer choice.

1 Which word correctly completes the sentence?

   The captain _____ the boat, and we all went to shore.

   A anchored
   B anckored
   C anshored
   D anghored

2 Which word correctly completes the sentence?

   We heard the students' _____ all the way down the hall.

   A lauchter
   B lauckter
   C lauphter
   D laughter

3 Which word correctly completes the sentence?

   My cousins were always involved in some sort of _____.

   A mitchief
   B mischief
   C misthief
   D misghief

4 Which word correctly completes the sentence?

   At the water park, we loved watching the _____ show.

   A dolthin
   B dolchin
   C dolghin
   D dolphin

Decoding

Grade 5, Unit 3: Revolution!

Name _____ Date _____

Lesson 13
WEEKLY TESTS 13.14

They Called Her Molly Pitcher
Decoding

5 Which word correctly completes the sentence?

   Jeri wanted to _____ some groceries at the store.

   A purthase
   B purshase
   C purckase
   D purchase

6 Which word correctly completes the sentence?

   Before the game, everyone sang the national _____.

   A anthem
   B anshem
   C anchem
   D anphem

7 Which word correctly completes the sentence?

   I played a _____ in the school play.

   A merckant
   B merchant
   C mershant
   D merghant

8 Which word correctly completes the sentence?

   I like your brother, _____ I sometimes get angry at him.

   A alchough
   B alshough
   C although
   D alghough

9 Which word correctly completes the sentence?

   The _____ threw the baseball to the batter.

   A pitther
   B pitsher
   C pitcher
   D pitcker

10 Which word correctly completes the sentence?

   We read a story about a bear cub who was an _____.

   A orthan
   B orphan
   C orghan
   D orchan

STOP

Decoding
© Houghton Mifflin Harcourt Publishing Company. All rights reserved.

Grade 5, Unit 3: Revolution!

Name _____ Date _____

Regular and Irregular Verbs

Lesson 13
WEEKLY TESTS 13.15

They Called Her Molly Pitcher
Language Arts

*D*irections
Use what you know about regular and irregular verbs to answer questions 1–10. For each question, circle the letter next to your answer choice.

1 Which word correctly completes the sentence?

   Lucinda _____ very hard to be nice to everyone.

   A trid
   B tried
   C have try
   D been tried

2 Which word correctly completes the sentence?

   I _____ a cake for you.

   A had bake
   B have baked
   C has been baked
   D have been baked

3 Which word correctly completes the sentence?

   Violet _____ a roller skating contest.

   A won
   B winned
   C have won
   D has winned

4 Which word correctly completes the sentence?

   Dora _____ to the train station with Stan.

   A came
   B comed
   C has comed
   D have came

Language Arts
© Houghton Mifflin Harcourt Publishing Company. All rights reserved.

Grade 5, Unit 3: Revolution!

Name _____ Date _____

Lesson 13
WEEKLY TESTS 13.16

They Called Her Molly Pitcher
Language Arts

5 Which word correctly completes the sentence?

> Teddy, what have you _____ today?

A ate
B aten
C eaten
D eated

6 Which word correctly completes the sentence?

> Jolie's little sister _____ last night.

A cryd
B cried
C have cried
D has been cryed

7 Which word correctly completes the sentence?

> Yesterday, Mr. Ripple _____ away all of the trash after the picnic.

A threw
B thrown
C throwd
D throwed

8 Which word correctly completes the sentence?

> I _____ that I had the correct answer.

A knew
B known
C knowed
D have known

9 Which word correctly completes the sentence?

> My twin and I _____ everybody when we dressed alike.

A surprisd
B surprised
C has surprised
D has been surprisd

10 Which word correctly completes the sentence?

> Yolanda _____ me a cup of juice.

A bringed
B brought
C has bringd
D have brought

STOP

Name _____ Date _____

Lesson 14
WEEKLY TESTS 14.1

James Forten
Test Record Form

TEST RECORD FORM	Possible Score	Criterion Score	Student Score
Vocabulary: Target Vocabulary, Greek and Latin Roots	10	8	
Comprehension: Sequence of Events, Selection Test	10	8	
Decoding: V V Syllable Pattern	10	8	
Language Arts: Active Voice and Passive Voice	10	8	
TOTAL	40	32	
		Total Student Score × 2.5 =	%

Test Record Form
© Houghton Mifflin Harcourt Publishing Company. All rights reserved.

Grade 5, Unit 3: Revolution!

Lesson 14
WEEKLY TESTS 14.2

Name _____ Date _____

James Forten
Vocabulary

Target Vocabulary, Greek and Latin Roots

Directions
Use what you know about the target vocabulary and Greek and Latin roots to answer questions 1–10. For each question, circle the letter next to your answer choice.

1 What does the word "aspects" mean in the sentence below?

> Lee solved all aspects of the problem.

A angles
B pledges
C entrances
D corrections

2 What does the word "persuade" mean in the sentence below?

> Dolores wanted to persuade her parents to let her grow a vegetable garden.

A burden
B instruct
C entertain
D convince

3 What does the word "tentative" mean in the sentence below?

> Wanda and her family made tentative plans to go on a picnic.

A with little food
B without preparation
C not fully worked out
D never done ahead of time

4 What does the word "apprentice" mean in the sentence below?

> Linda became a carpenter's apprentice.

A one who refuses to learn new things
B one who studies different kinds of plants
C one who keeps track of a business's money
D one who learns by watching an experienced worker

Go On

Vocabulary
© Houghton Mifflin Harcourt Publishing Company. All rights reserved.

Grade 5, Unit 3: Revolution!

Name _____ Date _____

Lesson 14
WEEKLY TESTS 14.3

James Forten
Vocabulary

5 What does the word "provisions" mean in the sentence below?

> The cowboys took all their provisions with them when they were on a cattle drive.

A coins
B friends
C supplies
D remarks

6 Which word **best** completes this sentence?

> We used a train to _____ the goods across the country.

A transject
B transport
C transgraph
D transmeter

7 Which word **best** completes this sentence?

> Kesha used a _____ to measure the outside temperature each morning.

A thermoject
B thermoport
C thermograph
D thermometer

8 Which word **best** completes this sentence?

> Nina and Dominic worked together on a science fair _____.

A project
B proport
C prograph
D prometer

9 Which word **best** completes this sentence?

> That is a beautiful _____ of Angel Falls.

A photoject
B photoport
C photograph
D photometer

10 Which word **best** completes this sentence?

> One _____ is smaller than one inch.

A centiject
B centiport
C centimeter
D centigraph

STOP

Vocabulary
© Houghton Mifflin Harcourt Publishing Company. All rights reserved.

Grade 5, Unit 3: Revolution!

Lesson 14
WEEKLY TESTS 14.4

Name _____ Date _____

James Forten
Comprehension

Sequence of Events, Selection Test

Directions
Think back to the selection "James Forten" to answer questions 1–10. For each question, circle the letter next to your answer choice.

1 Which event in the passage happens **first**?

   A James Forten is born.
   B James Forten goes to school.
   C Thomas Forten frees his wife.
   D Thomas Forten works making sails.

2 What is the **first** thing that Robert Bridges does when James is old enough to visit the sail shop?

   A sells the shop to James
   B lets James work around the shop doing odd jobs
   C pays to send James to a school created for African children
   D tells James he can't come around the shop until he gets an education

3 **Right after** Thomas Forten dies, James

   A is born
   B works on a ship
   C continues to go to school
   D gets permission to go to sea

4 Which of these does James's mother do **last**?

   A gives birth to a baby boy
   B gives James permission to go to sea
   C feels devastated by her husband's death
   D is freed when her husband earns enough money

5 **Right after** a cannonball is put into the gun barrel and pushed against the powder, the

   A powder is ignited
   B guns are reloaded
   C cannonballs shoot out of the gun
   D powder is tamped down by an assistant

6 What happens **before** James joins the crew of the *Royal Louis*?

   A James carries gunpowder to the guns.
   B The *Active* lowers its flags in surrender.
   C The ship sails out of Philadelphia.
   D James sees African captives on ships.

Go On

Comprehension

Grade 5, Unit 3: Revolution!

© Houghton Mifflin Harcourt Publishing Company. All rights reserved.

Lesson 14
WEEKLY TESTS 14.5

Name _____ Date _____

James Forten
Comprehension

7 James's third job was

A working at a small store
B carrying gunpowder to guns on a ship
C working with his father at the sail shop
D owning the business where his father had worked

8 Read the following events and place them in the order in which they appear in the selection.

1. The *Active* is sold.
2. The *Royal Louis* turns its prisoners over to military authorities.
3. The *Active* surrenders.
4. Decatur brings the *Royal Louis* back to Philadelphia.

A 4, 3, 1, 2
B 2, 1, 4, 3
C 3, 4, 2, 1
D 1, 4, 3, 2

9 What happens **after** the crew of the *Royal Louis* sights three British ships?

A The *Royal Louis* surrenders.
B The captain carefully checks the ship.
C The crew carries more gunpowder on board.
D The *Panoma* takes off for the island of Barbados.

10 The **last** thing that happens is that James

A is taken aboard the *Amphyon*
B becomes an apprentice to Robert Bridges
C plays marbles with a captain's son
D becomes the owner of his own business

Mark Student Reading Level:
___ Independent   ___ Instructional   ___ Listening

STOP

Comprehension
© Houghton Mifflin Harcourt Publishing Company. All rights reserved.

Grade 5, Unit 3: Revolution!

Name _____ Date _____

Lesson 14
WEEKLY TESTS 14.6

VV Syllable Pattern

James Forten
Decoding

Directions
Use what you know about the VV syllable pattern to complete sentences 1–10. For each question, circle the letter next to your answer choice.

1 If that spills, it will _____ my carpet.

  A ruin
  B ruan
  C roon
  D ruine

2 Sally's ancestors were _____.

  A pianeers
  B pieneers
  C pioneers
  D piuneers

3 In Washington there are many great _____.

  A museims
  B museems
  C museums
  D museams

4 Favio eats lots of fruit on his new _____.

  A deit
  B diet
  C diut
  D dyat

5 Penny did not _____ that the train had already left the station.

  A reilize
  B realize
  C reelize
  D reulize

6 I love going to the _____ to see a musical.

  A theater
  B thaeter
  C theeter
  D theuter

Go On

Decoding
© Houghton Mifflin Harcourt Publishing Company. All rights reserved.

Grade 5, Unit 3: Revolution!

Name _____ Date _____

Lesson 14
WEEKLY TESTS 14.7

James Forten
Decoding

7 We _____ all the things that our parents do for us.

A appreceite
B apprecyate
C appreceate
D appreciate

8 The necklace was made of _____ pearls.

A reil
B reel
C real
D reul

9 The children wanted to watch a _____.

A vidio
B video
C vidou
D vidyo

10 Today I go to my _____ lesson.

A piano
B pieno
C peano
D paino

STOP

Decoding

Grade 5, Unit 3: Revolution!

Name _____ Date _____

Lesson 14
WEEKLY TESTS 14.8

Active Voice and Passive Voice

James Forten
Language Arts

*D*irections
Use what you know about active voice and passive voice to answer questions 1–10. For each question, circle the letter next to your answer choice.

1 Which sentence is written using the ACTIVE VOICE?

  A The car is parked by my dad.
  B The toy was given to the baby.
  C Eloise gave me a new hairbrush.
  D Tony was greeted by his neighbor.

2 Which sentence is written using the ACTIVE VOICE?

  A The tickets were sold by the fifth graders.
  B Prizes were given to all the runners in the race.
  C Suzy and her sister giggle when they tell jokes.
  D The spelling bee was won by Todd and Arnold.

3 Which sentence is written using the ACTIVE VOICE?

  A Doug was invited by Calvin to the party.
  B The garage is where the car has been parked.
  C Patrice will give me the picture that she drew.
  D Grades for the test will be posted by the teacher.

4 Which sentence is written using the ACTIVE VOICE?

  A The students had fun dancing at the party.
  B The votes were counted by the committee.
  C The experiment was redone by the scientist.
  D The pond was where fishing and swimming were enjoyed.

Go On

Language Arts
© Houghton Mifflin Harcourt Publishing Company. All rights reserved.

Grade 5, Unit 3: Revolution!

Name _____ Date _____

Lesson 14
WEEKLY TESTS 14.9

James Forten
Language Arts

5 Which sentence is written using the ACTIVE VOICE?

  A Jim was thanked by his mother.
  B The doorbell was rung by the man.
  C Grandma came to visit us last week.
  D The math problem was solved by Ana.

6 Which sentence is written using the PASSIVE VOICE?

  A The dog likes to play in the backyard.
  B We watched the snow cover the ground.
  C Marci forgot to do her homework yesterday.
  D The pie was eaten by the family at the picnic.

7 Which sentence is written using the PASSIVE VOICE?

  A The trees were turning beautiful fall colors.
  B The horses trotted to the barn for some hay.
  C Dad wrote me ten letters while I was at camp.
  D Mistakes were made by players on both teams.

8 Which sentence is written using the PASSIVE VOICE?

  A The cat was taking a nap.
  B The toys were sold at the store.
  C The king likes to wear his crown.
  D The birds sang early this morning.

9 Which sentence is written using the PASSIVE VOICE?

  A Gretchen spoke in a whisper.
  B A child flew a kite in the park.
  C The leaves were raked by Alberto.
  D Time travel might be possible some day.

10 Which sentence is written using the PASSIVE VOICE?

  A Your truck was damaged by the fire.
  B The burglar ran away from the house.
  C The baby is still learning how to walk.
  D Lincoln was thinking about all he had to do.

STOP

Language Arts
© Houghton Mifflin Harcourt Publishing Company. All rights reserved.

Grade 5, Unit 3: Revolution!

Name _____ Date _____

Lesson 15
WEEKLY TESTS 15.1

We Were There, Too!
Test Record Form

TEST RECORD FORM	Possible Score	Criterion Score	Student Score
Vocabulary: Target Vocabulary, Prefixes *in-, im-, il-, ir-*	10	8	
Comprehension: Compare and Contrast, Selection Test	10	8	
Decoding: Vowel + /l/ Sounds in Unstressed Final Syllable	10	8	
Language Arts: Easily Confused Words	10	8	
TOTAL	40	32	

Total Student Score × 2.5 = _____ %

Go On

Test Record Form
© Houghton Mifflin Harcourt Publishing Company. All rights reserved.

Grade 5, Unit 3: Revolution!

Name _____ Date _____

Lesson 15
WEEKLY TESTS 15.2

Target Vocabulary, Prefixes
in-, im-, il-, ir-

We Were There, Too!
Vocabulary

Directions
Use what you know about the target vocabulary and prefixes to answer questions 1–10. For each question, circle the letter next to your answer choice.

1 What does the word "efficient" mean in the sentence below?

The students did an efficient job cleaning the park.

A taking their time
B working with others
C performing their best
D celebrating with honor

2 What does the word "organize" mean in the sentence below?

Joseph started to organize his toys on the bookshelf.

A order
B repair
C dispose
D magnify

3 What does the word "tedious" mean in the sentence below?

Delivering newspapers was a tedious job.

A humble
B tiresome
C marvelous
D reasonable

4 What does the word "mimic" mean in the sentence below?

Tory's little brother likes to mimic her.

A copy
B tease
C dazzle
D follow

Vocabulary
© Houghton Mifflin Harcourt Publishing Company. All rights reserved.

Grade 5, Unit 3: Revolution!

Name _____ Date _____

Lesson 15
WEEKLY TESTS 15.3

We Were There, Too!
Vocabulary

5 What does the word "peal" mean in the sentence below?

> There was a peal of laughter from the crowd.

A soft whisper
B loud sound
C grating noise
D sudden silence

6 What does the word "invisible" mean in the sentence below?

> The artist drew a picture with invisible ink.

A not seen before
B not able to be seen
C not written clearly
D not close enough to see

7 What does the word "impatient" mean in the sentence below?

> My uncle grew impatient while he waited for the bus.

A restless
B obedient
C confident
D desperate

8 What does the word "illegal" mean in the sentence below?

> It is illegal to drive through a red traffic light.

A not voting for a law
B not according to the law
C not understanding the law
D not a law that has been passed

Go On

Vocabulary

Lesson 15
WEEKLY TESTS 15.4

We Were There, Too!
Vocabulary

9 What does the word "irresponsible" mean in the sentence below?

The student knew she had been irresponsible when she lost her homework.

A not asking for help
B not taking one's time
C not keeping track of time
D not being careful with one's action

10 What does the word "impossible" mean in the sentence below?

The climbers thought it would be impossible to reach the top of the mountain.

A not paid attention
B not thought about
C not able to be done
D not given enough time

STOP

Vocabulary

Grade 5, Unit 3: Revolution!

Name _____ Date _____

Lesson 15
WEEKLY TESTS 15.5

We Were There, Too!
Comprehension

Compare and Contrast, Selection Test

*D*irections
Think back to the selection "We Were There, Too! Joseph Plumb Martin and Sybil Ludington" to answer questions 1–10. For each question, circle the letter next to your answer choice.

1 Joseph is different from his friends because he enlists

  A just for the money
  B almost by accident
  C sooner than the rest of them
  D when he is younger than they are

2 Continentals differ from militiamen in that

  A continentals are volunteer soldiers
  B militiamen get paid for their service
  C continentals are professional soldiers
  D militiamen always fight far from home

3 How does Joseph change between his first enlistment and his second?

  A He grows bored with fighting.
  B He feels proud to be a soldier.
  C He prefers to stay home and farm.
  D He likes to drill and march in parades.

4 How are Sybil and Paul Revere alike?

  A They both have a poem written about them.
  B They both travel forty miles during their rides.
  C They both get a postage stamp in their honor in 1975.
  D They both make brave rides to notify colonists about danger.

Go On

Comprehension
© Houghton Mifflin Harcourt Publishing Company. All rights reserved.

Grade 5, Unit 3: Revolution!

Name _____ Date _____

Lesson 15
WEEKLY TESTS 15.6

We Were There, Too!
Comprehension

5 How are Joseph and Sybil similar?

A They both own their own horse.
B They both work and live on farms.
C Their fathers are officers in the militia.
D Their actions help colonists defeat the British.

6 Joseph and Sybil are both

A happy to stay home and tend to their chores
B sorry they decide to get involved in the fight
C the same age when they first help the war effort
D willing to endure hardship to help ensure freedom

7 Sybil shows she is more interested than Joseph in fighting by

A watching men drill in the pasture
B riding farther than Paul Revere did
C writing a diary of the Revolutionary War
D volunteering to help notify soldiers to come fight

8 How can you tell that Joseph is less eager than Sybil to help the war effort?

A He is too young to enlist.
B He says he believes that he is a coward.
C He enlists for the shortest time possible.
D He hates to stay home while his friends go to war.

9 You can tell Sybil becomes more well-known than Joseph because

A Colonel Ludington is her father
B Alexander Hamilton marries her
C Paul Revere congratulates her on her ride
D George Washington thanks her personally

10 Joseph and Sybil both

A get married
B live to the age of ninety
C have bronze statues of themselves
D write books about their experiences

Mark Student Reading Level:
___ Independent ___ Instructional ___ Listening

STOP

Comprehension
© Houghton Mifflin Harcourt Publishing Company. All rights reserved.

Grade 5, Unit 3: Revolution!

Lesson 15
WEEKLY TESTS 15.7

Name _____ Date _____

We Were There, Too!
Decoding

Vowel + /l/ Sounds in Unstressed Final Syllable

*D*irections

Use what you know about vowel + /l/ sounds in unstressed final syllable to complete sentences 1–10. For each question, circle the letter next to your answer choice.

1 The coach blew the _____ at the end of the game.

   A whistal
   B whistil
   C whistul
   D whistle

2 Laura loves doing the crossword _____ in the Sunday newspaper.

   A puzzle
   B puzzil
   C puzzel
   D puzzul

3 Let's go look for _____.

   A fossils
   B fossles
   C fossols
   D fossels

4 Every time I hike on the mountain trail, I _____ and fall.

   A stumbil
   B stumbel
   C stumbul
   D stumble

5 My sister can easily thread the _____.

   A needil
   B needle
   C needel
   D needul

6 Tom used a _____ in his science experiment.

   A chemicil
   B chemicle
   C chemical
   D chemicul

Go On

Decoding
© Houghton Mifflin Harcourt Publishing Company. All rights reserved.

Grade 5, Unit 3: Revolution!

Name _____ Date _____

Lesson 15
WEEKLY TESTS 15.8

We Were There, Too!
Decoding

7 We shop at the _____ farmer's market.

   A locil
   B locle
   C local
   D locul

8 Has Steve read the newspaper _____ yet?

   A articil
   B articul
   C article
   D artical

9 My sister was dressed up to look like an _____ for the school play.

   A angil
   B angel
   C angal
   D angle

10 This rock is a type of _____.

   A minerle
   B minerel
   C minerul
   D mineral

STOP

Decoding

Grade 5, Unit 3: Revolution!

Easily Confused Words

Lesson 15
WEEKLY TESTS 15.9

We Were There, Too!
Language Arts

Directions
Use what you know about easily confused words to answer questions 1–10. For each question, circle the letter next to your answer choice.

1 Which sentence is written correctly?

   A Greg set a sack of feed in the barn.
   B Then Greg set on a stool to milk the cow.
   C His mother learn Greg to take care of the farm.
   D His mother does not leave Greg walk to school.

2 Which sentence is written correctly?

   A Pearl did a well job cleaning her room.
   B Pearl was having the worse day of her life.
   C It was the baddest storm Pearl had ever seen.
   D Dad told Pearl to have a good time at the library.

3 Which sentence is written correctly?

   A Grandma needs to lay down for a nap.
   B Our dog likes to lie by the foot of the bed.
   C The clerk had to rise the price of vegetables.
   D Norman watched the sun raise over the horizon.

4 Which sentence is written correctly?

   A Please leave Johnny come with me.
   B I will learn Johnny to chop firewood today.
   C Johnny and I will let first thing in the morning.
   D Johnny can teach me about different kinds of trees.

Go On

Lesson 15
WEEKLY TESTS 15.10

Name _____ Date _____

We Were There, Too!
Language Arts

5 Which sentence is written correctly?

A The parents will set in the audience to watch.
B Antonio already chose his two dancing partners.
C The sun will sit a little earlier each day all winter.
D Margie choose to sing a song at the school talent show.

6 Which sentence is written correctly?

A William ate less cereal than Angie.
B Fran drank least milk than she did yesterday.
C Mom gave the baby a little most time to play.
D Bethany scored the more points of all the players.

7 Which sentence is written correctly?

A Kelly hopes to get a raise at her job.
B The detective knew the burglar had laid.
C Sherry lied her books on the kitchen table.
D Every day, Eugene rises the flag at school.

8 Which sentence is written correctly?

A The football game has just began.
B The teams have begun to warm up.
C Did you see that player caught the ball?
D He almost catch the ball and ran a touchdown.

9 Which sentence is written correctly?

A Our class will learn how to grow a garden.
B The actors teached their lines to each other.
C We watched the kittens playfully fought over a toy.
D The birds have fight over which one sits on the feeder.

10 Which sentence is written correctly?

A I took notes in our social studies class.
B Gregor's less favorite fruit was bananas.
C Nell taked pictures at the zoo yesterday.
D I paid least for lunch than I did yesterday.

STOP

Language Arts
© Houghton Mifflin Harcourt Publishing Company. All rights reserved.

Grade 5, Unit 3: Revolution!

Name _____ Date _____

Lesson 16
WEEKLY TESTS 16.1

Lunch Money
Test Record Form

TEST RECORD FORM	Possible Score	Criterion Score	Student Score
Vocabulary: Target Vocabulary, Foreign Words Used in English/Word Origins	10	8	
Comprehension: Author's Purpose, Selection Test	10	8	
Decoding: Word Parts and Inflectional Endings	10	8	
Language Arts: Adjectives	10	8	
TOTAL	40	32	

Total Student Score × 2.5 = _____ %

Test Record Form
© Houghton Mifflin Harcourt Publishing Company. All rights reserved.

Grade 5, Unit 4: What's Your Story?

Lesson 16
WEEKLY TESTS 16.2

Name _____ Date _____

Lunch Money
Vocabulary

Target Vocabulary, Foreign Words Used in English/Word Origins

Directions
Use what you know about the target vocabulary and foreign words used in English/word origins to answer questions 1–10. For each question, circle the letter next to your answer choice.

1 What does the word "mental" mean in the sentence below?

> Caleb had a mental picture of himself giving his speech.

A colorful
B detailed
C in a frame
D in the mind

2 What does the word "record" mean in the sentence below?

> Andrea set a new record by winning the race at the fastest speed.

A a promise made to the public
B a goal that will never be reached
C a statistic that has never been beaten
D a problem that has many different solutions

3 What does the word "episodes" mean in the sentence below?

> My grandparents used to listen to episodes of a story that was told on the radio.

A parts
B legends
C questions
D discussions

4 What does the word "developed" mean in the sentence below?

> Marta developed the schedule for her soccer team.

A planned
B released
C destroyed
D condensed

Go On

Vocabulary
© Houghton Mifflin Harcourt Publishing Company. All rights reserved.

Grade 5, Unit 4: What's Your Story?

Lesson 16
WEEKLY TESTS 16.3

Lunch Money
Vocabulary

5 What does the word "feature" mean in the sentence below?

> **Today's talent show will feature the fifth-grade students.**

A educate
B focus on
C appreciate
D consult with

6 Read the sentences below.

> **While Janine sang, the audience was silent. When she finished, the crowd stood up and clapped.**

How does the word root aud help the reader understand what "audience" means?

A aud means "stand"
B aud means "hear"
C aud means "finish"
D aud means "clap"

7 Read the sentences below.

> **The man broke off a fraction of the biscuit. His dog enjoyed eating the tasty piece.**

How does the word root fract help the reader understand what "fraction" means?

A fract means "break"
B fract means "dog"
C fract means "eat"
D fract means "enjoy"

8 Read the sentences below.

> **The cars went different directions at the junction. There was a stop sign where the two roads met.**

How does the word root junct help the reader understand what "junction" means?

A junct means "car"
B junct means "stop"
C junct means "join"
D junct means "road"

Vocabulary

Lesson 16
WEEKLY TESTS 16.4

Name _____ Date _____

Lunch Money
Vocabulary

9 Read the sentences below.

The plane transported the people over the ocean. The suitcases were carried in the cargo part of the plane.

How does the word root port help the reader understand what "transported" means?

A port means "part"
B port means "water"
C port means "people"
D port means "carry"

10 Read the sentences below.

The children said the poem from memory. They recalled all the words correctly.

How does the word root mem helps the reader understand what "memory" means?

A mem means "to speak"
B mem means "children"
C mem means "correct"
D mem means "mindful of"

STOP

Vocabulary

Grade 5, Unit 4: What's Your Story?

Name _____ Date _____

Lesson 16
WEEKLY TESTS 16.5

Author's Purpose, Selection Test

Lunch Money
Comprehension

*D*irections
Think back to the selection "Lunch Money" to answer questions 1–10. For each question, circle the letter next to your answer choice.

1. Why did the author write "Lunch Money"?

   A to teach
   B to inform
   C to entertain
   D to persuade

2. The author writes "Greg had set a sales goal for the first week" to show that Greg

   A is following a plan
   B uses math in real life
   C listens to his father's advice
   D has only enough comics for one week

3. How does the author show that Greg worked hard to produce "Chunky Comics"?

   A by listing the story titles that Greg used for his comics
   B by describing the jobs that Greg did to make the comics
   C by showing that Greg made money by selling his comics
   D by explaining how Greg came up with the name of his comics

4. Which part of the selection did the author write to show that Greg is completely focused on selling his books?

   A *Regular comic books were sort of tall. Also a little floppy. Not Greg's.*
   B *He chewed the warm bread and the soft cheese, but he didn't taste a thing.*
   C *He got to pick the name because he was the author of all the Chunky Comics stories.*
   D *Comic books had been part of Greg's life forever, mostly because of his dad's collection.*

5. The author of "Lunch Money" believes that Greg

   A is a good student
   B needs writing lessons
   C thinks things through
   D will sell all his comics

Comprehension
© Houghton Mifflin Harcourt Publishing Company. All rights reserved.

Grade 5, Unit 4: What's Your Story?

Lesson 16
WEEKLY TESTS 16.6

Name _____ Date _____

Lunch Money
Comprehension

6 Why does the author of "Lunch Money" write, "The idea of making and selling comic books had hit Greg like a KRAK! over the head from Superman himself"?

A to make Greg look foolish
B to tell how Greg uses comic books
C to compare Greg to a comic book hero
D to show that Greg had a sudden thought

7 Which sentence does the author use to show Greg's love of comic books?

A *That's what Greg called the comic books he'd been selling—units.*
B *Comic books had been part of Greg's life forever, mostly because of his dad's collection.*
C *The cover illustration was powerful, the inside pictures were strong, and the story was loaded with action.*
D *Back in third grade Greg had used his own money to buy india ink, dip pens, brushes, and paper at the art supply store.*

8 The author of "Lunch Money" thinks that

A hard work pays off
B kids should create comics
C Greg's father is a kid at heart
D Greg's comics will become famous

9 The author calls this story "Lunch Money" because

A Greg uses money from his sales to buy lunch
B kids can only buy Greg's comics during lunch
C Greg spends lunchtime thinking about his sales
D kids spend their lunch money to buy Greg's comics

10 Why did the author show the ten steps Greg used to make his comic books?

A to encourage others to produce their own small books
B to tell how Greg became interested in creating his own comics
C to explain how reading comic books helped Greg develop story lines
D to describe the process used to create a small book from one piece of paper

Mark Student Reading Level:
____ Independent ____ Instructional ____ Listening

STOP

Comprehension
Grade 5, Unit 4: What's Your Story?

Name _____ Date _____

Lesson 16
WEEKLY TESTS 16.7

Lunch Money
Decoding

Word Parts and Inflectional Endings

Directions
Use what you know about word parts and inflectional endings to answer questions 1–10. For each question, circle the letter next to your answer choice.

1 What is the base word for the word "beginning"?

- A beg
- B begin
- C ing
- D ginning

2 What is the base word for the word "upsetting"?

- A up
- B upset
- C set
- D setting

3 What is the base word for the word "dimmed"?

- A dime
- B imme
- C med
- D dim

4 What is the base word for the word "occurred"?

- A cured
- B occur
- C occu
- D occurr

5 What is the base word for the word "knitting"?

- A knite
- B tting
- C knitte
- D knit

6 As the music played, the children were _____ their fingers.

- A snaps
- B snapes
- C snaping
- D snapping

Decoding

© Houghton Mifflin Harcourt Publishing Company. All rights reserved.

Grade 5, Unit 4: What's Your Story?

Name _____ Date _____

Lesson 16
WEEKLY TESTS 16.8

Lunch Money
Decoding

7 The kitchen has already been

- **A** scrubed
- **B** scrubing
- **C** scrubbed
- **D** scrubbing

8 The boys did not know where the sound came from, but they kept

- **A** searchd
- **B** searched
- **C** searching
- **D** searcheding

9 Rick found the book to be very

- **A** compeling
- **B** compelling
- **C** comppeling
- **D** comppelling

10 I asked my teacher if I could read a different book, but my request was

- **A** denyed
- **B** denied
- **C** denid
- **D** dennied

STOP

Name _____ Date _____

Adjectives

Lesson 16
WEEKLY TESTS 16.9

Lunch Money
Language Arts

*D*irections
Use what you know about adjectives to answer questions 1–10. For each question, circle the letter next to your answer choice.

1 Which ADJECTIVE describes the underlined noun?

> The American builder constructed a new house with French <u>windows</u> and wooden floors.

A American
B new
C French
D wooden

2 Which ADJECTIVE describes the underlined noun?

> The old man told fascinating <u>stories</u> about the unique history of each wonderful treasure in his shop.

A old
B fascinating
C unique
D wonderful

3 Which ADJECTIVE describes the underlined noun?

> Jamal went in the back room and counted sixteen <u>boxes</u> of kites on the rusty metal shelves.

A back
B sixteen
C rusty
D metal

4 Which ADJECTIVE describes the underlined noun?

> The <u>puppy</u> was very cute as it tracked muddy paw prints on the kitchen floor and chased a stuffed toy.

A cute
B muddy
C kitchen
D stuffed

Language Arts
© Houghton Mifflin Harcourt Publishing Company. All rights reserved.

Grade 5, Unit 4: What's Your Story?

Lesson 16
WEEKLY TESTS 16.10

Name _____ Date _____

Lunch Money
Language Arts

5 Which NOUN does the underlined adjective describe?

> A beautiful butterfly would soon emerge from the tiny cocoon and fly to a location in another country.

A cocoon
B butterfly
C location
D country

6 Which NOUN does the underlined adjective describe?

> Many Japanese tourists journey across the vast ocean to see the American landscapes in our national parks.

A tourists
B ocean
C landscapes
D parks

7 Which NOUN does the underlined adjective describe?

> The students were hungry as they entered the noisy cafeteria after studying for their math test.

A students
B cafeteria
C math
D test

8 What does the underlined adjective identify?

> My uncle showed us his German toys he had from when he was growing up.

A how many
B comparison
C what kind
D origin

9 What does the underlined adjective identify?

> My cousin is attending the largest Austin school.

A how many
B comparison
C what kind
D origin

10 What does the underlined adjective identify?

> I rode the Santa Fe Railroad with three of my best friends.

A origin
B what kind
C comparison
D how many

STOP

Name _____ Date _____

Lesson 17
WEEKLY TESTS 17.1

LAFFF
Test Record Form

TEST RECORD FORM	Possible Score	Criterion Score	Student Score
Vocabulary: Target Vocabulary, Using Reference Sources	10	8	
Comprehension: Story Structure, Selection Test	10	8	
Decoding: Recognizing Common Word Parts	10	8	
Language Arts: Adverbs	10	8	
TOTAL	40	32	

Total Student Score × 2.5 = ____ %

Test Record Form
© Houghton Mifflin Harcourt Publishing Company. All rights reserved.

Grade 5, Unit 4: What's Your Story?

Name _____   Date _____

Lesson 17
WEEKLY TESTS 17.2

Target Vocabulary, Using Reference Sources

LAFFF
Vocabulary

*D*irections
Use what you know about the target vocabulary and using a dictionary and a thesaurus to answer questions 1–10. For each question, circle the letter next to your answer choice.

1 What does the word "admitted" mean in the sentence below?

> Larry admitted that he did not read the directions on the box.

A pleaded
B squeaked
C confessed
D remembered

2 What does the word "impressed" mean in the sentence below?

> The teacher was impressed by how well the students presented their research reports.

A pleased
B surprised
C confused
D entertained

3 What does the word "original" mean in the sentence below?

> Carlos did research to find out who the original owner of the car was.

A odd
B first
C gentle
D lonely

4 What does the word "produced" mean in the sentence below?

> The farmer produced the largest and sweetest watermelons.

A ate
B sold
C grew
D inspected

Go On

Vocabulary
© Houghton Mifflin Harcourt Publishing Company. All rights reserved.

Grade 5, Unit 4: What's Your Story?

Name _____ Date _____

Lesson 17
WEEKLY TESTS 17.3

LAFFF
Vocabulary

5 What does the word "destination" mean in the sentence below?

> **The train was about an hour late when it finally reached its destination.**

A the place it was going
B the supplies it had stored
C the suitcases it left behind
D the passengers it was picking up

6 Read this dictionary entry for the word "award."

> **award** \ə-wôrd′\ *verb* **1.** to give by a judge **2.** to grant a prize *noun* **3.** a decision made by a judge **4.** a prize

Which definition represents the meaning of "award" as it is used in the following sentence?

> **The mayor gave the students an award for their recycling program.**

A Definition 1
B Definition 2
C Definition 3
D Definition 4

7 Read this dictionary entry for the word "project."

> **project** \prə jĕkt′\ *verb*
> **1.** to propose a plan of action
> **2.** to throw forward **3.** to cause something to appear on a surface **4.** to think forward using one's imagination

Which definition represents the meaning of "project" as it is used in the following sentence?

> **Ms. Woodward used a special machine to project the picture on the wall.**

A Definition 1
B Definition 2
C Definition 3
D Definition 4

Vocabulary
© Houghton Mifflin Harcourt Publishing Company. All rights reserved.

Grade 5, Unit 4: What's Your Story?

Name _____ Date _____

Lesson 17
WEEKLY TESTS 17.4

LAFFF
Vocabulary

8 Read this thesaurus entry for the word "mighty."

> **mighty** *adjective*: heroic, high, powerful, vast

Which word from the entry could be used in place of the word "mighty" as it is used in the following sentence?

The villagers could hear the mighty lion roar.

A vast
B high
C heroic
D powerful

9 Read this thesaurus entry for the word "soil."

> **soil** *noun:* country, dirt, home, region

Which word from the entry could be used in place of the word "soil" as it is used in the following sentence?

The farmer planted the seeds in the field's fertile soil.

A dirt
B home
C region
D country

10 Read the glossary entries.

> **desert** land with little or no rain
> **grassland** land where the natural plant life is mostly grass
> **temperate forest** a woodland with a mild climate and heavy rainfall
> **tropical rainforest** a woodland with over 100 inches of rain each year and many broad-leaved evergreen trees
> **tundra** a place with a cold climate that has a level or rolling plain without any trees

Which word from the glossary refers to a place that is cold and has no trees?

A desert
B tundra
C grassland
D tropical rainforest

STOP

Vocabulary

Name _____ Date _____

Lesson 17
WEEKLY TESTS 17.5

Story Structure, Selection Test

LAFFF
Comprehension

Directions
Think back to the selection "LAFFF" to answer questions 1–10. For each question, circle the letter next to your answer choice.

1 The **first** thing we learn in "LAFFF" is

A what Peter looks like
B what advice the Lus gave the Tangs
C that Peter and Angela go to the same school
D that Angela lives two doors down from Peter

2 What is the **first** important event in the story?

A Angela goes forward in time.
B Angela wins the story contest.
C Peter wears a costume like other kids.
D Peter shows Angela the time machine.

3 What happens at the school assembly?

A The kids in the class feel sorry for Angela.
B The principal punishes Angela for cheating.
C Angela thinks she stole someone else's story.
D Peter sends Angela into the future to get her story.

4 Peter changes how the kids feel about him by

A sharing his invention
B proving that he is a genius
C scaring Angela with a strange voice
D dressing up in an impressive costume

5 How does Angela learn about Peter's secret?

A She sees him in the future.
B She peeks in his garage window.
C She asks him what he is making.
D She tells him to bring her back a rose.

6 Peter helps Angela learn that

A the future is scary
B she is a good writer
C nothing will last forever
D she can be in two places at once

Comprehension
© Houghton Mifflin Harcourt Publishing Company. All rights reserved.

Grade 5, Unit 4: What's Your Story?

Name _____ Date _____

Lesson 17
WEEKLY TESTS 17.6

LAFFF
Comprehension

7 Who is the narrator of this story?

A Peter
B Angela
C Mrs. Tang
D Dr. Zweistein

8 The **main** conflict in the story is that

A Peter has no friends and studies all the time
B Angela has to walk to the bus with Peter every day
C Angela thinks her writing is not good enough to win a contest
D Peter's time machine sends things back to the future too quickly

9 How is the **main** conflict resolved?

A Peter repairs his time machine.
B Angela does not enter the story contest.
C Angela learns an important lesson by going into the future.
D Peter begins to talk with other kids and starts to make friends.

10 How is the ending of this story "circular"?

A Angela steals her own story.
B The story ends where it began.
C Peter goes back to being quiet.
D Everything works out for the characters.

Mark Student Reading Level:

___ Independent   ___ Instructional   ___ Listening

STOP

Comprehension

© Houghton Mifflin Harcourt Publishing Company. All rights reserved.

Grade 5, Unit 4: What's Your Story?

Lesson 17
WEEKLY TESTS 17.7

LAFFF
Decoding

Name _____ Date _____

Recognizing Common Word Parts

*D*irections
Use what you know about common word parts to answer questions 1–10. For each question, circle the letter next to your answer choice.

1 What does the word "undecided" mean in the sentence below?

   Susan was undecided about going to the movies.

   A will decide
   B decided again
   C will never decide
   D could not decide

2 What does the word "disagreed" mean in the sentence below?

   Steve and Sally disagreed about which book was better.

   A will never agree
   B did not agree
   C always agreed
   D should not agree

3 What does the word "unaware" mean in the sentence below?

   Holly was unaware that it was supposed to rain today.

   A not aware
   B aware again
   C aware before
   D sometimes aware

4 What does the word "reentered" mean in the sentence below?

   When Rufus reentered the room, everyone looked at him.

   A entered later
   B entered again
   C has not entered
   D one who entered

5 What does the word "displeasing" mean in the sentence below?

   The sound of the trumpet was displeasing to my ears.

   A not pleasing
   B very pleasing
   C always pleasing
   D sometimes pleasing

6 What does the word "refueled" mean in the sentence below?

   The pilot refueled the plane at the airport.

   A fueled now
   B cannot fuel
   C never fueled
   D fueled again

Decoding
© Houghton Mifflin Harcourt Publishing Company. All rights reserved.

Grade 5, Unit 4: What's Your Story?

Lesson 17
WEEKLY TESTS 17.8

Name _____ Date _____

LAFFF
Decoding

7 What does the word "unsupported" mean in the sentence below?

> **Because the block tower was unsupported, it came tumbling down.**

A not supported
B supported later
C supported again
D always supported

8 What does the word "unprepared" mean in the sentence below?

> **Marcy was unprepared to play the role.**

A not prepared
B prepared later
C always prepared
D will never be prepared

9 What does the word "reassigned" mean in the sentence below?

> **The homework was reassigned on Tuesday.**

A assigned now
B assigned later
C assigned again
D assigned before

10 What does the word "inactive" mean in the sentence below?

> **The turtle was inactive while it slept.**

A not active
B active again
C overly active
D active before

STOP

Decoding
© Houghton Mifflin Harcourt Publishing Company. All rights reserved.

Grade 5, Unit 4: What's Your Story?

Name _____ Date _____

Lesson 17
WEEKLY TESTS 17.9

Adverbs

LAFFF
Language Arts

*D*irections
Use what you know about adverbs to answer questions 1–10. For each question, circle the letter next to your answer choice.

1 Which word in the sentence is an ADVERB?

   The enormous crowd of runners was almost at the finish line.

   A enormous
   B crowd
   C runners
   D almost

2 Which word in the sentence is an ADVERB?

   As the elegant dancer moved gracefully, the soft music filled the room.

   A elegant
   B moved
   C gracefully
   D soft

3 Which word in the sentence is an ADVERB?

   Daryl said, "Sometimes you have to learn a difficult lesson and make a fresh start."

   A Daryl
   B Sometimes
   C difficult
   D fresh

4 Which word in the sentence is an ADVERB?

   The rain stopped, so the children started to play cheerfully.

   A stopped
   B the
   C cheerfully
   D play

Language Arts
© Houghton Mifflin Harcourt Publishing Company. All rights reserved.

Grade 5, Unit 4: What's Your Story?

Lesson 17
WEEKLY TESTS 17.10

Name _____ Date _____

LAFFF
Language Arts

5 Which word in the sentence is an ADVERB?

Suki met monthly with other students who were interested in rockets.

A met
B monthly
C other
D interested

6 Which word does the underlined adverb describe?

The neighbor gladly baked us an apple pie.

A neighbor
B baked
C apple
D pie

7 Which word does the underlined adverb describe?

The lion walked painfully on the paw with a thorn in it.

A walked
B paw
C thorn
D it

8 Which word does the underlined adverb describe?

The belt fit loosely around the baby's waist.

A belt
B fit
C the
D waist

9 Which word does the underlined adverb describe?

This type of bird is rarely seen in the wild.

A type
B of
C bird
D seen

10 Which word does the underlined adverb describe?

The clever dog swam safely to the shore.

A clever
B dog
C swam
D shore

STOP

Language Arts
© Houghton Mifflin Harcourt Publishing Company. All rights reserved.

Grade 5, Unit 4: What's Your Story?

Name _____ Date _____

Lesson 18
WEEKLY TESTS 18.1

The Dog Newspaper
Test Record Form

TEST RECORD FORM	Possible Score	Criterion Score	Student Score
Skills in Context: Fact and Opinion, Target Vocabulary	10	8	
Vocabulary: Target Vocabulary, Analogies	10	8	
Comprehension: Fact and Opinion, Selection Test	10	8	
Phonics: Recognizing Suffixes	10	8	
Language Arts: Prepositions and Prepositional Phrases	10	8	
TOTAL	50	42	
		Total Student Score × 2 =	%

- -

Test Record Form
© Houghton Mifflin Harcourt Publishing Company. All rights reserved.

Grade 5, Unit 4: What's Your Story?

Fact and Opinion, Target Vocabulary

The Dog Newspaper
Skills in Context

Directions Read the selection. Then read each question that follows the selection. Decide which is the best answer to each question. For each question, circle the letter next to your answer choice.

Dear Diary

Sunday, October 5

What a weekend! I had a wonderful time yesterday at the park. I watched three soccer games in a row. It was really exciting when the Yellow Jackets won the whole tournament!

I think the entire fifth grade was there, cheering the team on. Even Principal Shaffer came. Now, though, I have homework to do and my chores to finish before supper. Today, my mother asked that I fold the clean laundry and take out the trash before I do anything else. I'd better get moving.

Wednesday, October 8

Today, Ms. Tilden asked my class to write reports. We have four weeks to finish our reports. We are <u>required</u> to work in teams of three. Our <u>grade</u> is based on the report, so each team member gets the same grade.

Go On

Name _____ Date _____

The Dog Newspaper
Skills in Context

I am happy with my team because it was easy to choose roles. Yari loves to do research. She will find the books we need. I am a fast reader, so I will go through what she brings us. I will make notes about our topic. Seth loves to write. He puts information together in an interesting way. We will all help proofread. We will check for things like grammar and spelling. It might just be fun!

Saturday, October 18

My desk is piled with books. I hope I can find all the background information we need about marine life in the Pacific Ocean. We will need a lot of facts for our report. It looks like I will be too busy to write in my diary for the next couple of weeks.

Wednesday, November 5

I am actually looking forward to an <u>uneventful</u> weekend. I am glad there is nothing going on because I need to rest! Who knew writing a report with two other people would be such a challenge? Still, we had a great time working together. Seth is so funny! When we got worried about getting done on time, he would come out with a silly poem or riddle to make Yari and me laugh. We think we will get a good grade. We KNOW we were relieved to turn it in today. Writing that report was like running a marathon!

Sunday, November 9

I almost got my wish for a restful weekend, but I am glad I did not. Mom surprised me with a treat. She said I have been working hard for a long time. She was so proud of me that she wanted to reward me for being such a good student. Guess what we did? We drove two hours to my grandparents' house for a visit!

I love going to the country. Grandma had freshly baked pumpkin bread waiting when we pulled up. Grandpa told me I was getting smarter every day. He says that every time he sees me. Still, it makes me feel good. When we left, they promised to come to our house soon. I cannot wait!

Thursday, November 20

I am on Cloud Nine! We made a 93 on our report! Ms. Tilden said that our teamwork was among the best in the class and that the report was well written and showed a lot of research. I am glad that ordeal is over and we will be getting back to our regular class schedule.

Tuesday, December 2

Seth and Yari have become two of my best friends. We learned a lot about whales, dolphins, and fish, as well as each other! We decided to make plans to get together over the winter break. I am curious to see if we can decide what to do

The Dog Newspaper
Skills in Context

as easily as we divided up the jobs for the report. At any rate, I know we will laugh and have a ton of fun.

Friday, December 12

This weekend Mom and I will begin what she calls deep cleaning to prepare the house for my grandparents' visit.

I think I will paint a landscape and hang it in the guest room. Grandpa and I always go bowling when they come. He is an amazing bowler; I think I have only beaten him three times. It is fun spending time with him, and Mom and Grandma love to cook together without us underfoot in the kitchen.

---

1 Which of these sentences from the selection states the narrator's **opinion**?

A *Even Principal Shaffer came.*
B *It was really exciting when the Yellow Jackets won the whole tournament!*
C *Today, I am supposed to fold the clean laundry and take out the trash.*
D *Now, though, I have homework to do and my household chores to finish before supper.*

2 What does the word "required" mean as used in the passage?

A done again
B imagined
C called for
D drawn

Go On

Name _____ Date _____

The Dog Newspaper
Skills in Context

3 Which of these sentences from the selection states the narrator's **opinion**?

  A *Seth is so funny!*
  B *We have four weeks to finish our reports.*
  C *Today, Ms. Tilden asked my class to write reports.*
  D *Our grade is based on the report, so each team member gets the same grade.*

4 Why is this selection presented as a diary?

  A to show that the author lived long ago
  B to tell what the author thinks and feels
  C to compare the author to her grandparents
  D to explain why the author struggles in school

5 Which word in "Yari loves to do research" indicates that the statement is an **opinion**?

  A loves
  B to
  C do
  D research

6 Which of the following **best** describes the narrator?

  A loves to do research
  B fast reader
  C tells jokes
  D loves to write

Name _____ Date _____

Lesson 18
WEEKLY TESTS 18.6

The Dog Newspaper
Skills in Context

7 Which word in "Still, we had a great time working together" indicates that the statement is an **opinion**?

A Still
B had
C great
D working

8 What does the word "uneventful" mean as used in the passage?

A a time when families get together
B a time when exciting things will occur
C a time when little or nothing will happen
D a time when two problems must be solved

9 Which of these is an **opinion** expressed by the narrator?

A Grandma baked pumpkin bread.
B The report was difficult to write.
C There is marine life in the Pacific Ocean.
D The group of students had Yari do the research.

10 Which of these sentences from the selection states a **fact** in the narrator's life?

A *We made a 93 on our report!*
B *I am glad that ordeal is over and we will be getting back to our regular class schedule.*
C *At any rate, I know we will laugh and have a ton of fun.*
D *He is an amazing bowler; I think I have only beaten him three times.*

STOP

Skills in Context
© Houghton Mifflin Harcourt Publishing Company. All rights reserved.

Grade 5, Unit 4: What's Your Story?

Lesson 18
WEEKLY TESTS 18.7

Name _____ Date _____

The Dog Newspaper
Vocabulary

Target Vocabulary, Analogies

*D*irections
Use what you know about the target vocabulary and analogies to answer questions 1–10. For each question, circle the letter next to your answer choice.

1 What does the word "destruction" mean in the sentence below?

The community fought against the destruction of the old building.

A the act of creating
B the act of repainting
C the act of tearing down
D the act of choosing furniture

2 What does the word "required" mean in the sentence below?

The teacher told his students that they were required to prepare a science fair project.

A elected
B obliged
C advised
D inclined

3 What does the word "career" mean in the sentence below?

Jamar wanted to select a career in which he could use his writing skills and talent.

A job
B plot
C boss
D treat

4 What does the word "formula" mean in the sentence below?

The formula for creating the special flavor is a closely guarded secret.

A recipe
B unique
C chart
D mystery

- -

Vocabulary

Grade 5, Unit 4: What's Your Story?

Lesson 18
WEEKLY TESTS 18.8

Name _____ Date _____

The Dog Newspaper
Vocabulary

5 What does the word "edition" mean in the sentence below?

> **My dad read this morning's edition of the newspaper.**

A detail
B bridle
C humor
D version

Use what you know about analogies to complete the analogies in questions 6–10.

6 *Division* is to *multiplication* as *subtraction* is to

A subject
B addition
C geometry
D mathematics

7 *Depart* is to *wait* as *rise* is to

A elevate
B leave
C drop
D stop

8 *Song* is to *music* as *sport* is to

A work
B tune
C game
D busy

9 *Opinion* is to *fact* as *provide* is to

A give
B take
C speak
D truth

10 *Ignore* is to *notice* as *agree* is to

A regard
B obtain
C differ
D approve

STOP

Vocabulary

Grade 5, Unit 4: What's Your Story?

Name _____   Date _____

Lesson 18
WEEKLY TESTS 18.9

Fact and Opinion, Selection Test

The Dog Newspaper
Comprehension

*D*irections

Think back to the selection "The Dog Newspaper" to answer questions 1–10. For each question, circle the letter next to your answer choice.

1 Which statement from the selection is a **fact**?

A Or, "Max's only excitement is his daily walk on the leash."
B One soldier tucked the puppy inside his jacket to keep him warm.
C As the soldiers fought to protect the free world, B.J. did his duty, too.
D B.J. seemed especially fond of the Raggedy Ann and Andy stories, which were favorites of mine as well.

2 The author expresses the **opinion** that

A soldiers found B.J. when he was a puppy
B B.J.'s life was as uneventful as other dogs' lives
C her Uncle Bill could not keep a dog at his college
D she wrote the "Dog Newspaper" when she was ten

3 Which word in the phrase "B.J. had a unique background" shows that it is an **opinion**?

A a
B had
C unique
D background

4 Which word in the sentence "The gingerbread house was absolutely breathtaking" shows that it is an **opinion**?

A was
B house
C gingerbread
D breathtaking

5 Which of the following is a **fact** from the selection?

A The washing machine came in a cardboard box.
B B.J. enjoyed sleeping in the basement of the author's house at night.
C The box gingerbread doghouse was beautiful.
D The author worked hard to create a new place she thought B.J. would like.

Comprehension
© Houghton Mifflin Harcourt Publishing Company. All rights reserved.

Grade 5, Unit 4: What's Your Story?

Name _____ Date _____

Lesson 18
WEEKLY TESTS 18.10

The Dog Newspaper
Comprehension

6 The selection states the **fact** that

- **A** the author's brother was in the army
- **B** the men were too busy to take care of B.J.
- **C** B.J. offered love and laughter to the lonely soldiers
- **D** no one in Germany wanted to take care of a dog

7 Which of these is an **opinion** expressed in the selection?

- **A** B.J. lived with the author's family.
- **B** Bill was discharged from the army.
- **C** Bill did not stay in Austin very long.
- **D** B.J. was overjoyed when Bill came home.

8 Which of these sentences from the selection states a **fact**?

- **A** The next issue was even worse.
- **B** B.J. still had not done anything newsworthy.
- **C** Issue number three was a publishing disaster.
- **D** Less than one month after its launch, the "Dog Newspaper" went out of business.

9 Which word in "I believed my writing career was over" indicates that the statement is an **opinion**?

- **A** my
- **B** over
- **C** career
- **D** believed

10 Which of these sentences from the selection clearly states a **fact**?

- **A** What was in it for them? Except for the first issue, not much.
- **B** I need exciting plots, unique information, and fresh insights.
- **C** He lived to be sixteen, a good long life for an orphaned puppy who entered the world during a wartime bombing.
- **D** B.J. took one more plane ride, from Minneapolis to Fresno, California, where my parents moved shortly after I got married.

Mark Student Reading Level:

____ Independent   ____ Instructional   ____ Listening

STOP

Comprehension
© Houghton Mifflin Harcourt Publishing Company. All rights reserved.

Grade 5, Unit 4: What's Your Story?

Name _____ Date _____

Lesson 18
WEEKLY TESTS 18.11

Recognizing Suffixes

The Dog Newspaper
Decoding

Directions
Use what you know about suffixes to answer questions 1–10. For each question, circle the letter next to your answer choice.

1 What is the base word for the word "happier"?

A hap
B happ
C happi
D happy

2 Which base word will change its spelling when the ending -er is added?

A deep
B early
C green
D bright

3 If the pavement had more ice than any other place, it was the

A icest
B iciest
C icyest
D icierest

4 Of the two mice, the brown one is

A smallr
B smaler
C smaller
D smallerest

5 Which word has the suffix -est correctly added?

A thinest
B wideest
C smartest
D happyest

6 Which is the base word of the word "cozier"?

A cozy
B cozzi
C cozie
D cozzy

Decoding
© Houghton Mifflin Harcourt Publishing Company. All rights reserved.

Grade 5, Unit 4: What's Your Story?

Name _____ Date _____

Lesson 18
WEEKLY TESTS 18.12

The Dog Newspaper
Decoding

7 If John beat the other runners in the race, he was the

- **A** faster
- **B** fastter
- **C** fastest
- **D** fasterest

8 Of all the acts at the talent show, the last one was the

- **A** crazyer
- **B** craziest
- **C** crazyier
- **D** crazierest

9 The mother looked at her three children and knew whose room would be the

- **A** sloppier
- **B** sloppyer
- **C** sloppest
- **D** sloppiest

10 There were two trucks, but one was much

- **A** widr
- **B** wider
- **C** wideer
- **D** widder

STOP

Decoding

Grade 5, Unit 4: What's Your Story?

Name _____ Date _____

Lesson 18
WEEKLY TESTS 18.13

Prepositions and Prepositional Phrases

The Dog Newspaper
Language Arts

*D*irections
Use what you know about prepositions and prepositional phrases to answer questions 1–10. For each question, circle the letter next to your answer choice.

1 Which of the underlined words is a PREPOSITION?

The teacher asked <u>some</u> <u>of</u> the students to meet before <u>class</u>.

A some
B of
C the
D class

2 Which of the underlined words is a PREPOSITION?

I <u>remembered</u> <u>everything</u> except the keys <u>to</u> <u>my</u> house.

A remembered
B everything
C to
D my

3 Which of the underlined words is a PREPOSITION?

The <u>fifth</u> grade students <u>will</u> go <u>on</u> a field <u>trip</u> next Thursday.

A fifth
B will
C on
D trip

4 Which group of words is a PREPOSITIONAL PHRASE?

A took short naps
B under his window
C watched and waited
D walked quietly away

5 Which group of words is a PREPOSITIONAL PHRASE?

A between our houses
B a friend wrote
C my sister and I
D the new song

Language Arts
© Houghton Mifflin Harcourt Publishing Company. All rights reserved.

Grade 5, Unit 4: What's Your Story?

Name _____ Date _____

Lesson 18
WEEKLY TESTS 18.14

The Dog Newspaper
Language Arts

6 Which group of words is a PREPOSITIONAL PHRASE?

A and her sister
B will be copying
C threw the ball
D near the lake

7 What is the function of the underlined preposition?

My mother moved some of her plants <u>inside</u> because she expected cold weather.

A conveys purpose
B conveys time
C conveys location
D provides details

8 What is the function of the underlined preposition?

The map says we should next walk <u>toward</u> the tallest tree.

A conveys direction
B conveys time
C conveys purpose
D provides details

9 What is the function of the underlined prepositional phrase?

The horses trotted <u>with their owner</u> to the grassy field.

A conveys direction
B conveys time
C conveys location
D provides details

10 What is the function of the underlined prepositional phrase?

We had to wait in the line <u>for over three hours</u>.

A conveys purpose
B conveys time
C conveys location
D provides details

STOP

Language Arts
© Houghton Mifflin Harcourt Publishing Company. All rights reserved.

Grade 5, Unit 4: What's Your Story?

Name _____ Date _____

Lesson 19
WEEKLY TESTS 19.1

Darnell Rock Reporting
Test Reord Form

TEST RECORD FORM	Possible Score	Criterion Score	Student Score
Vocabulary: Target Vocabulary, Greek and Latin Suffixes -ist, -ism, -able, -ible	10	8	
Comprehension: Persuasion, Selection Test	10	8	
Decoding: More Common Suffixes	10	8	
Language Arts: More Kinds of Pronouns	10	8	
TOTAL	40	32	|//		Total Student Score × 2.5 =	%

Test Record Form

© Houghton Mifflin Harcourt Publishing Company. All rights reserved.

Grade 5, Unit 4: What's Your Story?

Name _____ Date _____

Lesson 19
WEEKLY TESTS 19.2

Darnell Rock Reporting
Vocabulary

Target Vocabulary, Greek and Latin Suffixes
-ist, -ism, -able, -ible

Directions
Use what you know about the target vocabulary and Greek and Latin suffixes to answer questions 1–10. For each question, circle the letter next to your answer choice.

1 What does the word "effective" mean in the sentence below?

Tommy was an effective group leader.

A good at producing results
B tired at the end of the day
C nervous in front of an audience
D selfish when asked to share with others

2 What does the word "granted" mean in the sentence below?

Our biggest wish was granted when we landed our spaceship safely on the moon.

A flung
B given
C affected
D dismissed

3 What does the word "urged" mean in the sentence below?

Wendy urged the scared puppy to come to her.

A coaxed
B elected
C humored
D disguised

4 What does the word "ordinance" mean in the sentence below?

The people voted for the new ordinance.

A city law
B natural disaster
C imaginary friend
D division problem

Go On

Vocabulary
© Houghton Mifflin Harcourt Publishing Company. All rights reserved.

Grade 5, Unit 4: What's Your Story?

Name _____ Date _____

Lesson 19
WEEKLY TESTS 19.3

Darnell Rock Reporting
Vocabulary

5 What does the word "minimum" mean in the sentence below?

   All of the students ran the minimum distance of two miles.

   A least
   B easiest
   C horrible
   D generous

6 Which choice **best** completes this sentence?

   The young boy dreamed of becoming a _____.

   A scientist
   B scientism
   C scientible
   D scientable

7 Which choice **best** completes this sentence?

   The firefighter was given a medal for her _____.

   A heroist
   B heroism
   C heroible
   D heroable

8 Which choice **best** completes this sentence?

   My sister is _____ to playing soccer.

   A agreent
   B agreeant
   C agreeist
   D agreeable

9 Which choice **best** completes this sentence?

   The students thought the homework assignment was _____.

   A managent
   B managant
   C manageism
   D manageable

10 Which choice **best** completes this sentence?

   The color of the butterfly matched the leaf, making it almost _____.

   A invisible
   B invisient
   C invisiant
   D invisibilist

STOP

Vocabulary
© Houghton Mifflin Harcourt Publishing Company. All rights reserved.

Grade 5, Unit 4: What's Your Story?

Name _____ Date _____

Persuasion, Selection Test

Lesson 19
WEEKLY TESTS 19.4

Darnell Rock Reporting
Comprehension

*D*irections
Think back to the selection "Darnell Rock Reporting" to answer questions 1–10. For each question, circle the letter next to your answer choice.

1 The **main** purpose of Darnell's article in the *South Oakdale Journal* is to persuade readers that

A gardens can be helpful
B homeless people need gardens
C a garden would help Sweeby Jones
D a garden should be built instead of a parking lot

2 Which is the **main** argument Darnell makes to persuade people to support building a garden?

A Nobody will be homeless anymore.
B Homeless people will not go hungry.
C Homeless people will take action to change their lives.
D Students will learn from the homeless people and join them.

3 The purpose of Linda's article is to persuade readers that

A teachers work hard
B she is smarter than Darnell
C homeless people cannot raise food
D a parking lot should be built for teachers

4 Linda uses all of the following arguments to support her position except

A homeless people can be harmful to students
B homeless people have no farming experience
C teachers are important and deserve to be supported
D teachers are better role models for students than homeless people

5 Darnell uses the quote "And if you don't mind people being hungry, then there is something wrong with you" to appeal to the

A reader's logic
B reader's emotions
C city council's logic
D city council's emotions

Go On

Comprehension
© Houghton Mifflin Harcourt Publishing Company. All rights reserved.

Grade 5, Unit 4: What's Your Story?

Name _____ Date _____

Lesson 19
WEEKLY TESTS 19.5

Darnell Rock Reporting
Comprehension

6 Which argument does Darnell use to help convince people that a garden would help people improve their own lives?

A The community should donate property for a garden.
B Students could learn to grow food for homeless people.
C Homeless people can grow food to eat or sell to make money.
D Teachers would prefer to have fresh vegetables instead of a parking lot.

7 A good argument against Linda's position could be that teachers

A already have a big parking lot
B are not that important to the students
C have money and can park in public lots
D would rather see students studying than gardening

8 What did the builder say to try to convince the city council that he did not intend to violate the building ordinance?

A He measured wrong.
B A mistake was made.
C The lot was too small.
D The ordinance was unfair.

9 Darnell believes that a garden would help students by

A keeping kids from messing up
B growing healthy food for them to eat
C encouraging them to work for someone else
D teaching them they can do something to help themselves

10 Which argument does Sweeby Jones make in support of Darnell's position?

A He is not involved with the school.
B Nobody has to think about the homeless people.
C The council does not have to answer his questions.
D Having a friend like Darnell might have made a difference in his life.

Mark Student Reading Level:
___ Independent   ___ Instructional   ___ Listening

STOP

More Common Suffixes

Lesson 19
WEEKLY TESTS 19.6

Darnell Rock Reporting
Decoding

Directions
Use what you know about suffixes to complete sentences 1–10. For each question, circle the letter next to your answer choice.

1 Luke went to town for an eye doctor ___

   A appointly
   B appointful
   C appointness
   D appointment

2 The students in the classroom were working ___

   A noisy
   B noisily
   C noiseful
   D noisement

3 That type of snake is ___

   A harmy
   B harmly
   C harmless
   D harmment

4 Jake will forgive my ___

   A forgetless
   B forgetness
   C forgetfully
   D forgetfulness

5 Mom and Dad had Doug and Sue sign a chore ___

   A agreeful
   B agreeable
   C agreeness
   D agreement

6 After our dog heard a strange noise, he was very ___

   A watchly
   B watchful
   C watchless
   D watchness

Go On

Decoding
© Houghton Mifflin Harcourt Publishing Company. All rights reserved.

Grade 5, Unit 4: What's Your Story?

Name _____ Date _____

Lesson 19
WEEKLY TESTS 19.7

Darnell Rock Reporting
Decoding

7 Ming was surprised by her own

   A clumsily
   B clumsiful
   C clumsiness
   D clumsiment

8 We could finally tell where the last player hid by the sound of her

   A movety
   B movely
   C moveful
   D movement

9 This autumn the days have been marked by

   A cloudily
   B cloudiful
   C cloudiness
   D cloudiment

10 After all Tim's company was gone, he felt

   A lonely
   B loneful
   C loneness
   D lonement

STOP

Decoding

Grade 5, Unit 4: What's Your Story?

Lesson 19
WEEKLY TESTS 19.8

Name _____ Date _____

More Kinds of Pronouns

Darnell Rock Reporting
Language Arts

Directions
Use what you know about pronouns to answer questions 1–10. For each question, circle the letter next to your answer choice.

1 Which word is an INDEFINITE PRONOUN?

   Cherie will give something special to her cousin.

   A will
   B something
   C her
   D cousin

2 Which word is an INDEFINITE PRONOUN?

   The theater has a few tickets left to sell.

   A theater
   B has
   C few
   D left

3 Which word is an INDEFINITE PRONOUN?

   Anyone who wants to come to our party is welcome.

   A anyone
   B who
   C wants
   D our

4 Which word is a POSSESSIVE PRONOUN?

   Mom and Dad were very proud of my exhibition.

   A were
   B very
   C proud
   D my

5 Which word is a POSSESSIVE PRONOUN?

   We do not know whose remarkable invention that is.

   A whose
   B remarkable
   C that
   D is

6 Which word is a POSSESSIVE PRONOUN?

   The view was theirs to appreciate every evening.

   A view
   B theirs
   C appreciate
   D evening

Go On

Language Arts
© Houghton Mifflin Harcourt Publishing Company. All rights reserved.

Grade 5, Unit 4: What's Your Story?

Name _____ Date _____

Lesson 19
WEEKLY TESTS 19.9

Darnell Rock Reporting
Language Arts

7 Which word is a POSSESSIVE PRONOUN?

> Last week we had to find a replacement for our bookkeeper.

A we
B find
C for
D our

8 Which word is an INTERROGATIVE PRONOUN?

> Which chemicals should we mix together to do the experiment?

A Which
B should
C we
D do

9 Which word is an INTERROGATIVE PRONOUN?

> What is the name of the Texas state official?

A What
B the
C Texas
D official

10 Which word is an INTERROGATIVE PRONOUN?

> When the phone rang, Mom looked at us and asked, "Who could that possibly be?"

A when
B us
C asked
D Who

STOP

Language Arts

Grade 5, Unit 4: What's Your Story?

Name _____ Date _____

Lesson 20
WEEKLY TESTS 20.1

Don Quixote and the Windmills
Test Record Form

TEST RECORD FORM	Possible Score	Criterion Score	Student Score
Vocabulary: Target Vocabulary, Idioms	10	8	
Comprehension: Understanding Characters, Selection Test	10	8	
Decoding: Stress in Three-Syllable Words	10	8	
Language Arts: Contractions	10	8	
TOTAL	40	32	
		Total Student Score × 2.5 =	%

Go On

Test Record Form
© Houghton Mifflin Harcourt Publishing Company. All rights reserved.

Grade 5, Unit 4: What's Your Story?

Name _____ Date _____

Lesson 20
WEEKLY TESTS 20.2

Target Vocabulary, Idioms

Don Quixote and the Windmills
Vocabulary

*D*irections
Use what you know about the target vocabulary and idioms to answer questions 1–10. For each question, circle the letter next to your answer choice.

1 What does the word "plagued" mean in the sentence below?

   During our picnic, we were plagued by flies.

   A joined
   B visited
   C bothered
   D entertained

2 What does the word "transformed" mean in the sentence below?

   The robot was transformed into a car.

   A lifted
   B stuffed
   C thrown
   D changed

3 What does the word "ignorance" mean in the sentence below?

   The man did not want to show his ignorance, so he did not say anything.

   A high fever
   B bad temper
   C great concern
   D poor knowledge

4 What does the word "antique" mean in the sentence below?

   The lamp was an antique.

   A made to work using oil
   B made hundreds of years ago
   C made after electricity was invented
   D made from different kinds of materials

5 What does the word "exploits" mean in the sentence below?

   My mom loves to tell about her exploits in the Navy.

   A great deeds
   B loyal friends
   C difficult jobs
   D interesting travels

Vocabulary
© Houghton Mifflin Harcourt Publishing Company. All rights reserved.

Grade 5, Unit 4: What's Your Story?

Lesson 20
WEEKLY TESTS 20.3

Name _____ Date _____

Don Quixote and the Windmills
Vocabulary

6 What does this sentence mean?

It is raining cats and dogs.

A There is a lot of rain.
B The rain is just beginning.
C The rain is coming in large drops.
D There is snow mixed with the rain.

7 What does this sentence mean?

The car can stop on a dime.

A The car can stop easily.
B The car can stop quietly.
C The car can stop slowly.
D The car can stop quickly.

8 What does this sentence mean?

The boys do not see eye to eye.

A The boys do not agree.
B The boys do not have fun.
C The boys do not see each other.
D The boys do not know each other.

9 What does this sentence mean?

The girl is in hot water.

A The girl is in trouble.
B The girl is having fun.
C The girl is taking a bath.
D The girl is studying for a test.

10 What does this sentence mean?

Mindy is as sharp as a tack.

A Mindy is silly.
B Mindy is smart.
C Mindy is angry.
D Mindy is jealous.

STOP

Vocabulary
© Houghton Mifflin Harcourt Publishing Company. All rights reserved.

Grade 5, Unit 4: What's Your Story?

Name _____ Date _____

Lesson 20
WEEKLY TESTS 20.4

Understanding Characters, Selection Test

Don Quixote and the Windmills
Comprehension

*D*irections
Think back to the selection "Don Quixote and the Windmills" to answer questions 1–10. For each question, circle the letter next to your answer choice.

1 When Señor Quexada changes his name to Don Quixote, it indicates that he

  A forgot his real name
  B does not like his name
  C lives in a fantasy world
  D wants to hide his real identity

2 When Don Quixote puts on a rusted suit of armor, the reader understands that he is

  A like a child playing dress-up
  B going to have true adventures
  C continuing a great family tradition
  D a knight with an important mission

3 Why does Sancho Panza agree to be Don Quixote's squire?

  A He loves to read about knights.
  B He is as unrealistic as Don Quixote.
  C He thinks it will be fun to see the world.
  D He wants his wife to be queen of an island.

4 Don Quixote's heart "overflowed with devotion" when he whispered Dulcinea's name because she was

  A dying
  B his wife
  C completely devoted to him
  D his lady and he was her knight

5 Whom does the reader believe, and why, when Don Quixote and Sancho Panza disagree about the figures they see in the distance?

  A Don Quixote, because he is a knight
  B Sancho Panza, because he always has to be right
  C Don Quixote, because he believes in giants and spells
  D Sancho Panza, because he knows what they really are

Comprehension
© Houghton Mifflin Harcourt Publishing Company. All rights reserved.

Grade 5, Unit 4: What's Your Story?

Lesson 20
WEEKLY TESTS 20.5

Don Quixote and the Windmills
Comprehensive

Name _____ Date _____

6 When Sancho questions the attack on the windmills, Don Quixote becomes irritated because he

A is convinced his enemy has sent giants to kill him
B thinks that Sancho is afraid he will not get an island
C believes that Sancho does not understand his mission
D knows that the giants are bewitched to look like windmills

7 The words that **best** describe Sancho Panza are

A greedy and lazy
B realistic and loyal
C scared and doubting
D reckless and arrogant

8 Don Quixote's **main** goal is to

A conquer the world
B fulfill his fondest fantasies
C make Dulcinea proud of him
D live his life as a brave knight

9 What is Sancho's attitude at the end of the story?

A He vows to follow Don Quixote wherever he goes.
B He decides to go back home to his wife and children.
C He fears that Don Quixote's fantasies will get them both killed.
D He begins to see things the same way that Don Quixote sees them.

10 The reader can tell from Don Quixote's character that the word "quixotic" means all of these except

A rational
B unpredictable
C in search of ideals
D foolishly impractical

Mark Student Reading Level:
___ Independent ___ Instructional ___ Listening

STOP

Comprehension
Grade 5, Unit 4: What's Your Story?

Name _____ Date _____

Lesson 20
WEEKLY TESTS 20.6

Stress in Three-Syllable Words

Don Quixote and the Windmills
Decoding

Directions
Use what you know about stress in three-syllable words to read sentences 1–10. Choose the answer that correctly shows which syllable of the underlined word is stressed. For each question, circle the letter next to your answer choice.

1. The mosquito buzzed in my ear.

   A MOS • qui • to
   B mos • QUI • to
   C mos • qui • TO
   D MOS • qui • TO

2. Ralph looked like a cowboy in his bandanna.

   A BAN • dan • na
   B ban • DAN • na
   C ban • DAN • NA
   D BAN • DAN • na

3. José and Irma like to sit on the patio.

   A pat • i • O
   B pat • I • O
   C PAT • i • o
   D PAT • I • O

4. Diedre was happy to play her tambourine with the others.

   A tam • bour • INE
   B TAM • bour • ine
   C tam • BOUR • ine
   D TAM • BOUR • ine

5. I will bring a tomato from my garden for the salad.

   A to • MA • to
   B TO • ma • to
   C to • ma • TO
   D TO • ma • TO

6. Casey ate vanilla ice cream.

   A VA • nil • la
   B va • nil • LA
   C va • NIL • la
   D va • NIL • LA

Decoding
© Houghton Mifflin Harcourt Publishing Company. All rights reserved.

Grade 5, Unit 4: What's Your Story?

Lesson 20
WEEKLY TESTS 20.7

Name _____ Date _____

Don Quixote and the Windmills
Decoding

7 Tino got new striped <u>pajamas</u>.

A pa • jam • AS
B pa • JAM • as
C pa • JAM • AS
D PA • jam • as

8 We visited that <u>cathedral</u> in Italy.

A CA • the • dral
B ca • THE • dral
C ca • the • DRAL
D ca • THE • DRAL

9 Theo is eating a <u>burrito</u> for lunch.

A BUR • ri • to
B bur • ri • TO
C bur • RI • to
D BUR • RI • TO

10 My favorite scene is when the hero stops the <u>stampeding</u> cattle.

A stam • PED • ing
B STAM • ped • ing
C STAM • PED • ing
D stam • ped • ING

STOP

Decoding
© Houghton Mifflin Harcourt Publishing Company. All rights reserved.

Grade 5, Unit 4: What's Your Story?

Name _____ Date _____

Lesson 20
WEEKLY TESTS 20.8

Contractions

Don Quixote and the Windmills
Language Arts

Directions
Use what you know about contractions to replace the underlined word or words in sentences 1–10. For each question, circle the letter next to your answer choice.

1 They are monitoring the average daily temperature as part of their experiment.

  A They're
  B They'are
  C They'r
  D The'yr

2 The travelers cannot stop the caravan of camels.

  A cann't
  B can't
  C ca'not
  D can'nt

3 The flower will not bloom for another few days.

  A wo'nt
  B willn't
  C won't
  D will'nt

4 We could not finish the construction of the doghouse because of the rainstorm.

  A could't
  B couldn't
  C couln't
  D could'nt

5 I think he will give you a postage stamp for your letter.

  A he'l
  B hew'll
  C h'ill
  D he'll

6 We are going to the university first.

  A We're
  B We'r
  C W'are
  D W're

Language Arts
© Houghton Mifflin Harcourt Publishing Company. All rights reserved.

Grade 5, Unit 4: What's Your Story?

Don Quixote and the Windmills
Language Arts

7 She has had a miserable day because her car broke down.

A Sheh's
B She's
C She'is
D She'as

8 Brad thinks they will need more kerosene for the lantern.

A they'l
B they'ill
C they'll
D the'will

9 The picture we have drawn will be shown in a book produced by students.

A we've
B we'hv
C we'ave
D w've

10 The superintendent says she will give the award to the students.

A she'ill
B she'l
C shel'l
D she'll

Name _____ Date _____

Lesson 21
WEEKLY TESTS 21.1

Tucket's Travels
Test Record Form

TEST RECORD FORM	Possible Score	Criterion Score	Student Score
Vocabulary: Target Vocabulary, Synonyms	10	8	
Comprehension: Sequence of Events, Selection Test	10	8	
Decoding: Common Final Syllables	10	8	
Language Arts: The Verbs *be* and *have*	10	8	
TOTAL	40	32	

Total Student Score × 2.5 = _____ %

Test Record Form
© Houghton Mifflin Harcourt Publishing Company. All rights reserved.

Grade 5, Unit 5: Under Western Skies

Name _____ Date _____

Target Vocabulary, Synonyms

Lesson 21
WEEKLY TESTS 21.2

Tucket's Travels
Vocabulary

Directions
Use what you know about the target vocabulary and synonyms to answer questions 1–10. For each question, circle the letter next to your answer choice.

1 What does the word "seep" mean in the sentence below?

> The water will seep through the rocks to create a natural spring.

A dry
B flow
C stir
D throb

2 What does the word "evident" mean in the sentence below?

> The solution to the mystery was evident.

A barely known
B easily understood
C quickly dismissed
D slowly recognized

3 What does the word "salvation" mean in the sentence below?

> The cat's salvation was assured when the firefighter pulled him from the tree.

A the state of taking a nap
B the state of playing a game
C the state of being saved from harm
D the state of being taken on a journey

4 What does the word "undoubtedly" mean in the sentence below?

> The boy undoubtedly could run very fast.

A hardly
B probably
C certainly
D desperately

Go On

Vocabulary
© Houghton Mifflin Harcourt Publishing Company. All rights reserved.

Grade 5, Unit 5: Under Western Skies

Name _____ Date _____

Lesson 21
WEEKLY TESTS 21.3

Tucket's Travels
Vocabulary

5 What does the word "pace" mean in the sentence below?

> The elephant's pace can be very fast if it is frightened.

A life
B sleep
C walk
D measure

6 Read the thesaurus entry below for the word "goal."

> **goal** *noun*: aim, dream, plan, target

Which word from the entry could be used in place of the word "goal" as it is used in the following sentence?

> The player scored 6 points by reaching the goal.

A aim
B plan
C dream
D target

7 Read the thesaurus entry below for the word "hail."

> **hail** *verb*: cheer, come, greet, name

Which word from the entry could be used in place of the word "hail" as it is used in the following sentence?

> I heard that our new neighbors hail from Scotland.

A come
B cheer
C greet
D name

8 Read the thesaurus entry below for the word "consider."

> **consider** *verb*: believe, judge, hold, study

Which word from the entry could be used in place of the word "consider" as it is used in the following sentence?

> The detective will consider all of the facts before drawing a conclusion.

A hold
B judge
C study
D believe

Vocabulary

Grade 5, Unit 5: Under Western Skies

Lesson 21
WEEKLY TESTS 21.4

Name _____ Date _____

Tucket's Travels
Vocabulary

9 Read the thesaurus entry below for the word "subject."

> **subject** *noun*: case, chapter, class, customer

Which word from the entry could be used in place of the word "subject" as it is used in the following sentence?

> **Reading is Debbie's favorite subject in school.**

A case
B class
C chapter
D customer

10 Read the thesaurus entry below for the word "appeal."

> **appeal** *noun*: plea, charm
> *verb*: beg, attract

Which word from the entry could be used in place of the word "appeal" as it is used in the following sentence?

> **Brad will appeal to his parents to go on the camping trip.**

A beg
B plea
C charm
D attract

STOP

Vocabulary

Grade 5, Unit 5: Under Western Skies

Name _____ Date _____

Lesson 21
WEEKLY TESTS 21.5

Tucket's Travels
Comprehension

Sequence of Events, Selection Test

Directions
Think back to the selection "Tucket's Travels" to answer questions 1–10. For each question, circle the letter next to your answer choice.

1 Which of the following events takes place **first** in the selection?

A Francis carries Billy.
B Lottie and Billy's father dies.
C Francis finds Lottie and Billy alone.
D Lottie and Billy are abandoned by their wagon train.

2 **Before** Francis finds Lottie and Billy,

A Grimes helps them escape
B Francis brushes out their footprints
C Francis searches for his own family
D the Comancheros track Grimes

3 Which of the following events takes place **last** in the selection?

A The Pawnee kidnap Francis.
B Grimes teaches Francis how to survive.
C The Comancheros follow Grimes and the mules.
D Francis leads the children across the hot, dusty plains.

4 Nearly every time Francis and the children see water and trees, they

A drink the water
B also see a herd of buffalo
C realize they are imagining things
D see the Comancheros coming for them

5 Billy falls sound asleep

A during the storm
B while Francis carries him
C before Francis carries him
D after Francis puts him down

6 **After** Francis tells Lottie to dig, Lottie

A sees a mirage
B digs and finds water
C digs and finds nothing
D sees the dust from the Comancheros

Comprehension
© Houghton Mifflin Harcourt Publishing Company. All rights reserved.

Grade 5, Unit 5: Under Western Skies

Name _____ Date _____

Lesson 21
WEEKLY TESTS 21.6

Tucket's Travels
Comprehension

7 What do Francis and the children do **after** the bolt of lightning hits close to them?

A They wake Billy up.
B They drink fresh water.
C They take cover under a ledge.
D They run for the shelter of the trees.

8 What is the first thing Francis does **after** the storm?

A goes into the sun
B stretches his legs
C looks toward the west
D takes off his buckskin shirt

9 **After** the storm, Francis and the children appear

A frightened
B well rested
C muddy and wet
D refreshed and happy

10 Francis is relieved **after** the heavy rainfall because

A they are all safe
B Lottie and Billy are safe
C their footprints are gone
D the Comancheros are lost

Mark Student Reading Level:
____ Independent ____ Instructional ____ Listening

STOP

Comprehension
© Houghton Mifflin Harcourt Publishing Company. All rights reserved.

Grade 5, Unit 5: Under Western Skies

Name _____ Date _____

Lesson 21
WEEKLY TESTS 21.7

Common Final Syllables

Tucket's Travels
Decoding

Directions
Use what you know about common final syllables to answer questions 1–10. For each question, circle the letter next to your answer choice.

1. What is the base word of the word "pleasure"?

   A pleased
   B pleasu
   C please
   D pleasing

2. What is the base word of the word "furniture"?

   A furn
   B furnishings
   C furnish
   D furnit

3. What is the base word of the word "departure"?

   A depart
   B depar
   C departu
   D parture

4. What is the base word of the word "mixture"?

   A mix
   B mixing
   C mixt
   D mixtu

5. What is the base word of the word "natural"?

   A natu
   B nature
   C natur
   D nurture

6. What is the final syllable of the word "fashion"?

   A ashion
   B shion
   C ion
   D hion

Decoding
© Houghton Mifflin Harcourt Publishing Company. All rights reserved.

Grade 5, Unit 5: Under Western Skies

Name _____ Date _____

Lesson 21
WEEKLY TESTS 21.8

Tucket's Travels
Decoding

7 What is the final syllable of the word "surgeon"?

A eon
B on
C geon
D urgeon

8 What is the final syllable of the word "horizon"?

A on
B rizon
C izon
D zon

9 What is the final syllable of the word "certain"?

A in
B ain
C tain
D rtain

10 What is the final syllable of the word "caption"?

A ion
B on
C ption
D tion

STOP

Name _____ Date _____

Lesson 21
WEEKLY TESTS 21.9

The Verbs *be* and *have*

Tucket's Travels
Language Arts

Directions
Use what you know about the verbs *be* and *have* to answer questions 1–10. For each question, circle the letter next to your answer choice.

1 Which word **best** completes the sentence below?

> **This is the first time Tommy _____ grown green beans in his garden.**

  A is
  B has
  C was
  D have

2 Which word **best** completes the sentence below?

> **I _____ the tallest student in my class.**

  A is
  B am
  C are
  D were

3 Which word **best** completes the sentence below?

> **Yesterday, Manny and Sheryl _____ ten newspapers left over.**

  A has
  B had
  C was
  D were

4 Which word **best** completes the sentence below?

> **They _____ often traveled to Padre Island National Seashore to go to the beach.**

  A has
  B was
  C have
  D were

Language Arts
© Houghton Mifflin Harcourt Publishing Company. All rights reserved.

Grade 5, Unit 5: Under Western Skies

Lesson 21
WEEKLY TESTS 21.10

Name _____ Date _____

Tucket's Travels
Language Arts

5 Which word **best** completes the sentence below?

There _____ a crack in the vase.

A is
B am
C are
D were

6 Which word **best** completes the sentence below?

Zane and Kris _____ planning to come to the meeting.

A is
B am
C was
D were

7 Which word **best** completes the sentence below?

There _____ twelve months in the year.

A is
B has
C are
D have

8 Which word **best** completes the sentence below?

Everett _____ learned how to use a telescope.

A is
B has
C was
D have

9 Which word **best** completes the sentence below?

Wendy _____ fun at the art museum.

A are
B had
C have
D were

10 Which word **best** completes the sentence below?

Abe _____ walking along the beach with his mom.

A has
B was
C have
D were

STOP

Language Arts
© Houghton Mifflin Harcourt Publishing Company. All rights reserved.

Grade 5, Unit 5: Under Western Skies

Name _____ Date _____

Lesson 22
WEEKLY TESTS 22.1

The Birchbark House
Test Record Form

TEST RECORD FORM	Possible Score	Criterion Score	Student Score
Vocabulary: Target Vocabulary, Using Reference Sources	10	8	
Comprehension: Theme, Selection Test	10	8	
Decoding: More Final Syllables	10	8	
Language Arts: Perfect Tenses	10	8	
TOTAL	40	32	

Total Student Score × 2.5 = _____ %

Test Record Form
© Houghton Mifflin Harcourt Publishing Company. All rights reserved.

Grade 5, Unit 5: Under Western Skies

Name _____ Date _____

Lesson 22
WEEKLY TESTS 22.2

Target Vocabulary, Using Reference Sources

The Birchbark House
Vocabulary

Directions
Use what you know about the target vocabulary and using reference sources to answer questions 1–10. For each question, circle the letter next to your answer choice.

1 What does the word "deserted" mean in the sentence below?

> Mr. Smith cared for the chicks after they were deserted by their mother.

A captured
B prompted
C frightened
D abandoned

2 What does the word "nerve" mean in the sentence below?

> Amanda lost her nerve to sing in front of an audience.

A fear
B pain
C shame
D courage

3 What does the word "astonish" mean in the sentence below?

> The shooting stars streaking across the night sky will astonish the visitors.

A enclose
B surprise
C distress
D construct

4 What does the word "margins" mean in the sentence below?

> Pedro took notes in the margins of the story.

A questions about the print
B spaces between lines of print
C borders around a printed page
D blank pages before the print begins

Go On

Vocabulary
© Houghton Mifflin Harcourt Publishing Company. All rights reserved.

Grade 5, Unit 5: Under Western Skies

Name _____ Date _____

Lesson 22
WEEKLY TESTS 22.3

The Birchbark House
Vocabulary

5 What does the word "reasoned" mean in the sentence below?

> Naomi reasoned that she could walk the dog and play basketball before it got dark outside.

A hoped
B panicked
C admitted
D concluded

6 Read the dictionary entry below for the word "bind."

> **bind** \bīnd\ *verb* **1.** to tie **2.** to combine with **3.** to protect **4.** to bandage

Which definition represents the meaning of "bind" as it is used in the following sentence?

> The students will bind the bundle of newspapers with some twine.

A Definition 1
B Definition 2
C Definition 3
D Definition 4

7 Read the dictionary entry below for the word "craft."

> **craft** \craft\ *noun* **1.** skill in making or planning something **2.** a piece of art **3.** a boat, ship, or aircraft *verb* **4.** to make by hand

Which definition represents the meaning of "craft" as it is used in the following sentence?

> We boarded the craft in Galveston and sailed across the ocean.

A Definition 1
B Definition 2
C Definition 3
D Definition 4

8 Read the thesaurus entry below for the word "grant."

> **grant** *verb:* admit, give, transfer *noun:* gift

Which word from the entry could be used in place of the word "grant" as it is used in the following sentence?

> Harry applied for a grant to pay for summer camp.

A gift
B give
C admit
D transfer

Vocabulary
© Houghton Mifflin Harcourt Publishing Company. All rights reserved.

Grade 5, Unit 5: Under Western Skies

Name _____ Date _____

Lesson 22
WEEKLY TESTS 22.4

The Birchbark House
Vocabulary

9 Read the thesaurus entry below for the word "select."

> **select** *adjective:* favored
> *verb:* choose, elect, pick

Which word from the entry could be used in place of the word "select" as it is used in the following sentence?

> **April was one of a select group of students who were invited to the ceremony.**

A   pick
B   elect
C   choose
D   favored

10 Read the glossary entries below.

> **agriculture** farming
> **climate** the weather in an area over a period of time
> **crops** plants, such as grain, vegetables, or fruit
> **drought** a period of dry weather

Which word from the entries refers to weather without rainfall?

A   crops
B   climate
C   drought
D   agriculture

STOP

Vocabulary

Grade 5, Unit 5: Under Western Skies

Name _____ Date _____

Lesson 22
WEEKLY TESTS 22.5

Theme, Selection Test

The Birchbark House
Comprehension

*D*irections
Think back to the selection "The Birchbark House" to answer questions 1–10. For each question, circle the letter next to your answer choice.

1 Omakayas decides to eat the whole lump of maple candy because she

   A knows the bear cubs want it
   B wants to avoid tanning a moose hide
   C knows that Angeline does not like sweets
   D does not think it can be divided into pieces

2 How does Omakayas think she will impress Angeline?

   A She will help Angeline tan the moose hide.
   B She will tell Angeline that she hurt her feelings.
   C She will make Angeline beg to get some of the berries.
   D She will share the lump of maple candy with Angeline.

3 Why do the bear cubs suddenly back away from Omakayas?

   A They are afraid of her size.
   B Their mother shows up and slaps them.
   C Their mother pins her on the ground.
   D They are not hungry and do not want any berries.

4 The reason the mother bear attacks Omakayas is

   A to keep her cubs safe from humans
   B she smells bear grease on Omakayas's skin
   C she wants the berries that Omakayas picked
   D to show the cubs that humans should be killed

5 What does Omakayas learn from her moment with the mother bear?

   A fear
   B power
   C humor
   D respect

6 You can tell that the bear cubs respect their mother because they

   A give the berries back to Omakayas
   B bite on a stick that Omakayas wiggles
   C attack Omakayas when she cuts their mother's fur
   D leave Omakayas when their mother guides them away

Comprehension
© Houghton Mifflin Harcourt Publishing Company. All rights reserved.

Grade 5, Unit 5: Under Western Skies

Name _____ Date _____

Lesson 22
WEEKLY TESTS 22.6

The Birchbark House
Comprehension

7 What will the bear cubs **most likely** do the next time they see a person?

A go home with the person
B stay away from the person
C lead their mother to the person
D expect the person to feed them berries

8 How do you think Angeline will feel when she hears the story about Omakayas's day?

A angry
B jealous
C scornful
D relieved

9 Omakayas will **most likely**

A realize that Angeline is always right
B get in trouble with a mother bear again
C be more careful when she is dealing with nature
D try to find the bear cubs she thinks of as brothers

10 What is the theme of this selection?

A A true friend will always share.
B Good things come to those who wait.
C Family and friends come before adventure.
D It is important to respect the rules of the wild.

Mark Student Reading Level:
____ Independent ____ Instructional ____ Listening

STOP

Comprehension

Grade 5, Unit 5: Under Western Skies

Name _____ **Date** _____

Lesson 22
WEEKLY TESTS 22.7

More Final Syllables

The Birchbark House
Decoding

*D*irections

Use what you know about final syllables to answer questions 1–10. For each question, circle the letter next to your answer choice.

1 What is the base word of the word "service"?

   A serv
   B server
   C serve
   D servi

2 What is the base word of the word "passage"?

   A passa
   B pass
   C pas
   D passed

3 What is the base word of the word "creative"?

   A creat
   B creation
   C created
   D create

4 What is the base word of the word "notice"?

   A noti
   B note
   C noted
   D not

5 What is the base word of the word "justice"?

   A jus
   B just
   C justi
   D ice

6 What is the final syllable of the word "relative"?

   A ative
   B ive
   C lative
   D tive

Decoding
© Houghton Mifflin Harcourt Publishing Company. All rights reserved.

Grade 5, Unit 5: Under Western Skies

Lesson 22
WEEKLY TESTS 22.8

The Birchbark House
Decoding

Name _____ Date _____

7 What is the final syllable of the word "postage"?

  A tage
  B ge
  C age
  D stage

8 What is the final syllable of the word "creative"?

  A ve
  B ative
  C tive
  D ive

9 What is the final syllable of the word "cabbage"?

  A abbage
  B bbage
  C age
  D bage

10 What is the final syllable of the word "average"?

  A ge
  B age
  C erage
  D rage

STOP

Name _____ Date _____

Lesson 22
WEEKLY TESTS 22.9

Perfect Tenses

The Birchbark House
Language Arts

*D*irections
Use what you know about perfect tenses to complete sentences 1–10. For each question, circle the letter next to your answer choice.

1 Which words **best** complete the sentence below?

   Trudy _____ to speak Spanish.

   A had learnted
   B have learnt
   C has learned
   D will has learned

2 Which words **best** complete the sentence below?

   Lisa _____ a letter to the mayor.

   A has writed
   B has wroten
   C had written
   D have wroted

3 Which words **best** complete the sentence below?

   The children _____ the books they want to give to the library.

   A has brung
   B had brang
   C have brought
   D will have bringed

4 Which words **best** complete the sentence below?

   Our school choir _____ in a contest.

   A has sung
   B had sang
   C have singed
   D will have sungen

5 Which words **best** complete the sentence below?

   If all goes well, Eli _____ the race when the rain starts.

   A had finish
   B has finished
   C have finishd
   D will have finished

6 Which words **best** complete the sentence below?

   My brothers _____ to take out the garbage.

   A has forgot
   B had forgetted
   C have forgotten
   D will have forgotted

Language Arts
© Houghton Mifflin Harcourt Publishing Company. All rights reserved.

Grade 5, Unit 5: Under Western Skies

Name _____ Date _____

Lesson 22
WEEKLY TESTS 22.10

The Birchbark House
Language Arts

7 Which words **best** complete the sentence below?

> The outfielder _____ the ball!

A has caught
B has catched
C have catched
D have caughten

8 Which words **best** complete the sentence below?

> Aunt Beth, who was tired from her trip, _____ for ten hours.

A has slept
B had sleepen
C have sleeped
D will have sleept

9 Which words **best** complete the sentence below?

> The dog _____ to fetch the ball.

A had ran
B has run
C had runned
D has ranned

10 Which words **best** complete the sentence below?

> Mark _____ the house keys to his sister.

A has gived
B have gave
C had given
D will have give

STOP

Language Arts
© Houghton Mifflin Harcourt Publishing Company. All rights reserved.

Grade 5, Unit 5: Under Western Skies

Name _____ Date _____

Lesson 23
WEEKLY TESTS 23.1

Vaqueros: America's First Cowboys
Test Record Form

TEST RECORD FORM	Possible Score	Criterion Score	Student Score
Skills in Context: Main Ideas and Details, Target Vocabulary	10	8	
Vocabulary: Target Vocabulary, Word Families	10	8	
Comprehension: Main Ideas and Details, Selection Test	10	8	
Decoding: Unstressed Syllables	10	8	
Language Arts: Transitions	10	8	
TOTAL	50	40	

Total Student Score × 2 = _____ %

Test Record Form

Grade 5, Unit 5: Under Western Skies

Main Ideas and Details, Target Vocabulary

Vaqueros: America's First Cowboys
Skills in Context

Directions
Read the selection. Then read each question that follows the selection. Decide which is the best answer to each question. For each question, circle the letter next to your answer choice.

Today's Cowhands

When people imagine cowhands, they often visualize what they have observed in the movies. However, the ranching industry has altered significantly over the years. Long ago, ranches <u>extended</u> over vast areas, with cattle roaming over open ranges. Cowhands from various ranches would work together during roundups, branding the new calves and selling the older cattle.

Today's cowhands <u>acknowledge</u> that new inventions have made their jobs much less difficult. Most ranches are much smaller. The ranches also use barbed wire fences to keep the cattle from going astray, as they once did on the open range. Although cowhands continue to ride horses, they more often drive trucks around the ranches. Cattle can be transported from place to place using trains and large trailers, ensuring the trip to different regions of the country is much faster. Cowhands, who once spent lengthy periods of time on the trail with the cattle, can now spend more time at home with their families.

Even the cowhands' attire has transformed over time. Cowhands used to wear clothes that were discarded by other people. They wore any kind of hat with a wide brim that would prevent the sun from blinding their eyes. It was not until the 1900s that cowhands wore a felt hat, a large belt buckle, and pointed boots. Today's cowhands generally wear jeans, a brightly colored shirt, work boots, and a baseball cap. However, the felt hat remains a symbol of cowhand life.

Go On

How to Care for a Felt Cowhand Hat

Many cowhand hats are constructed from felt, a light and smooth fabric. Felt is made by using hot water and steam to press together short, single fibers. It is a terrific fabric for hats because it lasts a long time. To keep a felt cowhand hat looking good, there are some important steps to follow.

- Always place your hat on a flat surface. Turn it upside down so that it is resting on its crown, which is the top of the hat. Never rest it on its brim because the brim could be flattened and lose its shape.

- Avoid leaving your hat in a place that gets particularly hot, such as a heater. You should also avoid places that are humid, such as the bathroom when you are taking a shower.

- If the hat gets too hot or there is too much moisture in the air, the sweatband, which is the part that makes your hat fit your head, will likely shrink.

- Sometimes your sweatband will get wet from perspiration or your hat will get wet from bad weather, such as rain, sleet, or snow. If this happens, remove your hat, then flip up the sweatband in order to allow it to dry. This will stop the water from soaking into your hat. Wait for the sweatband or hat to air dry. Never try to rush the drying process by using something like a hair dryer. The heat will damage the hat.

Lesson 23
WEEKLY TESTS 23.4

Name _____ Date _____

Vaqueros: America's First Cowboys
Skills in Context

1 What does the word "extended" mean as used in the passage?

A attended
B patrolled
C stretched
D reflected

2 What does the word "acknowledge" mean as used in the passage?

A admit
B worry
C laugh
D suggest

3 How are today's ranches different from the ones long ago?

A They only raise sheep.
B They are smaller in size.
C They have more cowhands.
D They grow their own food.

4 Which detail from the selection supports the idea that cowhands who lived long ago did not have a lot of money?

A *However, the felt cowhand hat remains a symbol of cowhand life.*
B *Cowhands from various ranches would work together during roundups, branding the new calves and selling the older cattle.*
C *Cowhands used to wear clothes that were discarded by other people.*
D *When people imagine cowhands, they often visualize what they have observed in the movies.*

5 Why did cowhands used to wear hats with a wide brim?

A to keep the heat off their head
B to keep the sun out of their eyes
C to keep the dust out of their mouth
D to keep the tree branches away from their face

Go On

Skills in Context
© Houghton Mifflin Harcourt Publishing Company. All rights reserved.

Grade 5, Unit 5: Under Western Skies

Name _____ Date _____

Lesson 23
WEEKLY TESTS 23.5

Vaqueros: America's First Cowboys
Skills in Context

6 Read the diagram of information from the selection.

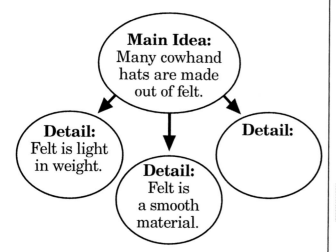

Which of these belongs in the empty circle?

A Felt costs very little.
B Felt lasts a long time.
C Felt comes in many colors.
D Felt stays dry in wet weather.

7 A cowhand should never rest a felt hat on its brim because the brim will

A tear
B bend
C shrink
D flatten

8 What should a cowhand do after the sweatband on a felt hat gets wet?

A Flip up the sweatband.
B Leave the sweatband alone.
C Use a hair dryer to dry the sweatband.
D Replace the sweatband with a new one.

9 What is this selection **mostly** about?

A cowhand foods
B cowhand stories
C modern cowhands
D famous cowhands

10 What is the **most likely** reason the author wrote this selection?

A to tell how cowhands talk
B to teach a lesson about cowhands
C to describe how cowhands care for cattle
D to convince people to become cowhands

STOP

Skills in Context
© Houghton Mifflin Harcourt Publishing Company. All rights reserved.

Grade 5, Unit 5: Under Western Skies

Name _____ Date _____

Lesson 23
WEEKLY TESTS 23.6

Target Vocabulary, Word Families

Vaqueros: America's First Cowboys
Vocabulary

*D*irections
Use what you know about the target vocabulary and word families to answer questions 1–10. For each question, circle the letter next to your answer choice.

1 What does the word "hostile" mean in the sentence below?

The desert is a hostile environment.

A not dry
B not quiet
C not scary
D not friendly

2 What does the word "decline" mean in the sentence below?

Javier noticed a sharp decline in last month's sales.

A debt
B delay
C defense
D decrease

3 What does the word "sprawling" mean in the sentence below?

The lava was sprawling over the volcano.

A burning
B spreading
C collecting
D operating

4 What does the word "prospered" mean in the sentence below?

The new store prospered by selling children's books.

A increased
B succeeded
C celebrated
D entertained

5 What does the word "acquainted" mean in the sentence below?

The new student got acquainted with his classmates.

A to know
B to study
C to discuss
D to practice

6 Which word belongs to the same word family as "conduct" and "product"?

A duck
B chuckle
C deduction
D spectacle

Go On

Vocabulary
© Houghton Mifflin Harcourt Publishing Company. All rights reserved.

Grade 5, Unit 5: Under Western Skies

Name _____ Date _____

Lesson 23
WEEKLY TESTS 23.7

Vaqueros: America's First Cowboys
Vocabulary

7 Which word belongs to the same word family as "transport" and "report"?

A porch
B export
C porcupine
D overnight

8 Which word belongs to the same word family as "biography" and "autograph"?

A craft
B gravity
C laughter
D photograph

9 Which word belongs to the same word family as "inspect" and "respect"?

A peck
B special
C peculiar
D spectacle

10 Which word belongs to the same word family as "memory" and "memorial"?

A more
B order
C medicine
D remember

STOP

Vocabulary

Grade 5, Unit 5: Under Western Skies

Main Ideas and Details, Selection Test

Lesson 23
WEEKLY TESTS 23.8

Vaqueros: America's First Cowboys
Comprehension

*D*irections

Think back to the selection "Vaqueros: America's First Cowboys" to answer questions 1–10. For each question, circle the letter next to your answer choice.

1 What is the section titled "The Journeys" **mostly** about?

A how the Totonac people welcomed Cortéz
B what explorers from Spain did in the Americas
C who supported Columbus's trips to the West Indies
D why Vera Cruz, Mexico, was once called New Spain

2 The Totonac people wanted to conquer the

A Aztecs
B Cubans
C Haitians
D Spaniards

3 Which animal did Coronado introduce to the American Southwest?

A wild horses
B pot-bellied pigs
C longhorn cattle
D mountain goats

4 Read the diagram of information from the selection.

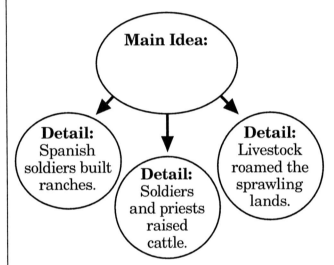

Which of these belongs in the empty circle?

A Vaqueros helped take care of the livestock.
B The Spanish king gave soldiers gifts of land.
C Catholic missionaries converted the native people.
D Coronado searched for the legendary Golden Cities.

Go On

Comprehension
© Houghton Mifflin Harcourt Publishing Company. All rights reserved.

Grade 5, Unit 5: Under Western Skies

Name _____ Date _____

Lesson 23
WEEKLY TESTS 23.9

Vaqueros: America's First Cowboys
Comprehension

5 A lasso is a

   A cow-man
   B cattle ranch
   C looped rope
   D native convert

6 The section entitled "Way of Life" is **mostly** about the daily life of

   A vaqueros
   B adventurers
   C Spanish kings
   D Catholic missionaries

7 Vaqueros wore *sombreros* to protect their

   A faces
   B legs
   C feet
   D hands

8 In 1821, New Spain became

   A Texas
   B Mexico
   C America
   D California

9 What is the **main** reason that vaqueros no longer needed to ride the wide-open spaces after the Civil War?

   A Ranches were reduced in size and had smaller herds of cattle.
   B Freed slaves and young men from the East became cowboys.
   C Barbed wire allowed ranchers to keep their cattle in fenced pastures.
   D Railroads were used to transport cattle to markets in eastern and western cities.

10 The last section, "Celebrating Traditions," is **mostly** about

   A corrals and barns
   B rodeos and charrerias
   C old and new haciendas
   D cowboys and native people

Mark Student Reading Level:
____ Independent   ____ Instructional   ____ Listening

Comprehension

Name _____ Date _____

Unstressed Syllables

Lesson 23
WEEKLY TESTS 23.10

Vaqueros: America's First Cowboys
Decoding

Directions
Use what you know about unstressed syllables to answer questions 1–10. For each question, circle the letter next to your answer choice.

1 What is the unstressed syllable in the word "talent"?

   A tal
   B len
   C ent
   D al

2 What is the unstressed syllable in the word "wisdom"?

   A sdom
   B wis
   C dom
   D wisd

3 What is the unstressed syllable in the word "dozen"?

   A ozen
   B doze
   C en
   D doz

4 What is the unstressed syllable in the word "adopt"?

   A a
   B ad
   C dop
   D opt

5 What is the unstressed syllable in the word "challenge"?

   A nge
   B chal
   C alle
   D lenge

6 What is the unstressed syllable in the word "kitchen"?

   A ki
   B en
   C kit
   D chen

Go On

Decoding

Grade 5, Unit 5: Under Western Skies

Name _____ Date _____

Lesson 23
WEEKLY TESTS 23.11

Vaqueros: America's First Cowboys
Decoding

7 What is the unstressed syllable in the word "surround"?

A ur
B ound
C round
D sur

8 What is the unstressed syllable in the word "frighten"?

A ten
B fri
C en
D ghte

9 What is the unstressed syllable in the word "question"?

A tion
B ques
C stion
D que

10 What is the unstressed syllable in the word "abode"?

A ab
B a
C obe
D bode

STOP

Decoding
© Houghton Mifflin Harcourt Publishing Company. All rights reserved.

Grade 5, Unit 5: Under Western Skies

Name _____ Date _____

Lesson 23
WEEKLY TESTS 23.12

Transitions

Vaqueros: America's First Cowboys
Language Arts

Directions
Use what you know about transitions to answer questions 1–10. For each question, circle the letter next to your answer choice.

1 Which of the underlined words in the sentence below is a TRANSITION word or phrase?

> Dad called from work and said he would be home soon.

A soon
B from
C called
D would

2 Which of the underlined words in the sentence below is a TRANSITION word or phrase?

> During the storm, the boat was anchored near the coast.

A coast
B storm
C During
D anchored

3 Which of the underlined words in the sentence below is a TRANSITION word or phrase?

> In conclusion, the officials decided to wait on passing the new rules.

A to wait on
B the officials
C the new rules
D In conclusion

4 Which of the underlined words in the sentence below is a TRANSITION word or phrase?

> Until the train leaves, Joe will wait here.

A will
B here
C Until
D leaves

Go On

Language Arts
Grade 5, Unit 5: Under Western Skies

Name _____ Date _____

Lesson 23
WEEKLY TESTS 23.13

Vaqueros: America's First Cowboys
Language Arts

5 Which of the underlined words in the sentence below is a TRANSITION word or phrase?

> **Finally, my brother and I got to go to the park to fly our kites.**

A our
B park
C Finally
D brother

6 Which of the underlined words in the sentence below is a TRANSITION word or phrase?

> **The baseball team won the game and, as a result, earned the prize.**

A as a result
B won the game
C earned the prize
D The baseball team

7 Which of the underlined words in the sentence below is a TRANSITION word or phrase?

> **The cowhands plan to ride across the range tomorrow.**

A ride
B across
C cowhands
D tomorrow

8 Which of the underlined words in the sentence below is a TRANSITION word or phrase?

> **Tara sang a song while she rode her bike to school.**

A her
B sang
C while
D school

Language Arts
© Houghton Mifflin Harcourt Publishing Company. All rights reserved.

Grade 5, Unit 5: Under Western Skies

Vaqueros: America's First Cowboys
Vocabulary

9 Which of the underlined words in the sentence below is a TRANSITION word or phrase?

> <u>As a result</u> of the storm, Pete learned <u>an important lesson</u> from his mom <u>about how to</u> repair <u>a tree house</u>.

A As a result
B a tree house
C about how to
D an important lesson

10 Which of the underlined words in the sentence below is a TRANSITION word or phrase?

> Julie <u>promised</u> that she <u>would</u> take <u>out</u> the garbage <u>next</u>.

A out
B next
C would
D promised

Name _____ Date _____

Lesson 24
WEEKLY TESTS 24.1

Rachel's Journal
Test Record Form

TEST RECORD FORM	Possible Score	Criterion Score	Student Score
Vocabulary: Target Vocabulary, Using Context	10	8	
Comprehension: Cause and Effect, Selection Test	10	8	
Decoding: Simple Prefixes	10	8	
Language Arts: Making Comparisons	10	8	
TOTAL	40	32	
		Total Student Score × 2.5 =	%

Test Record Form
© Houghton Mifflin Harcourt Publishing Company. All rights reserved.

Grade 5, Unit 5: Under Western Skies

Lesson 24
WEEKLY TESTS 24.2

Name _____ Date _____

Rachel's Journal
Vocabulary

Target Vocabulary, Using Context

Directions
Use what you know about the target vocabulary and using context to answer questions 1–10. For each question, circle the letter next to your answer choice.

1 What does the word "fared" mean in the sentence below?

> **Bob fared well when he competed in the track-and-field events.**

A dressed
B answered
C succeeded
D interpreted

2 What does the word "mishap" mean in the sentence below?

> **The baby had a mishap and spilled his milk.**

A permit
B scheme
C entrance
D accident

3 What does the word "balked" mean in the sentence below?

> **The horse balked when it came to the wooden jump.**

A refused to move
B looked confident
C jumped gracefully
D waited for permission

4 What does the word "disadvantage" mean in the sentence below?

> **The disadvantage of people not having wings is that we need machines to fly.**

A motto
B ransom
C drawback
D reputation

5 What does the word "lectured" mean in the sentence below?

> **The teacher lectured us about learning the safety rules.**

A talked sternly to
B operated quickly for
C manuevered solemnly with
D remarked rudely about

Go On

Vocabulary
© Houghton Mifflin Harcourt Publishing Company. All rights reserved.

Grade 5, Unit 5: Under Western Skies

Name _____ Date _____

Lesson 24
WEEKLY TESTS 24.3

Rachel's Journal
Vocabulary

6 What does the word "timid" mean in the sentence below?

> The timid dog was afraid of his own reflection in the mirror.

A deaf
B lazy
C playful
D fearful

7 What does the word "chamber" mean in the sentence below?

> After seeing all of the other rooms, the tourists finally entered the king's chamber in the castle.

A mold
B room
C district
D balcony

8 What does the word "ignored" mean in the sentence below?

> Kate ignored the noise of the train as it passed by, and she continued reading her book.

A was impressed by
B imitated the sound of
C refused to take notice of
D remembered to make a record of

9 What does the word "brisk" mean in the sentence below?

> The students took a brisk walk around the neighborhood, returning to their starting point in a short amount of time.

A quick
B boring
C casual
D formal

10 What does the word "operate" mean in the sentence below?

> I would like to learn how to operate a tractor because I think it would be fun to drive.

A work
B clean
C trade
D repair

STOP

Vocabulary

© Houghton Mifflin Harcourt Publishing Company. All rights reserved.

Grade 5, Unit 5: Under Western Skies

Name _____ Date _____

Lesson 24
WEEKLY TESTS 24.4

Rachel's Journal
Comprehension

Cause and Effect, Selection Test

Directions
Think back to the selection "Rachel's Journal" to answer questions 1–10. For each question, circle the letter next to your answer choice.

1 The rustling in the bushes that Rachel and the children hear at the beginning of the story is caused by

A an ox
B a storm
C a turkey
D an Indian

2 What causes Rachel's body to quake at the beginning of the story?

A fear
B illness
C happiness
D excitement

3 Rachel pretends to be brave because she

A likes to act
B wants to calm the children
C believes it is part of her adventure
D wants her parents to be proud of her

4 What happens when Rachel and the children climb to a high point when they are lost?

A They see their campfire.
B They find some Indians.
C They discover a new route.
D They sleep through a storm.

5 Rachel loses the privilege of taking cut-offs after lunch because

A the river is unsafe
B a storm is coming
C an Indian confronts her
D she and the children get lost

6 After an Indian is friendly to the children, they are

A captured by the Indian's tribe
B happy to introduce him to their parents
C required to stay close to the wagon train
D allowed to take cut-offs anytime they want

Go On

Comprehension
© Houghton Mifflin Harcourt Publishing Company. All rights reserved.

Grade 5, Unit 5: Under Western Skies

Lesson 24
WEEKLY TESTS 24.5

Name _____ Date _____

Rachel's Journal
Comprehension

7 What effect does rain have on the trail?

  A The trail is destroyed.
  B The trail is flooded and can't be used.
  C The trail becomes less dusty but very muddy.
  D The trail becomes a good path for the herd of cattle.

8 What causes the ferry to break loose from its moorings?

  A rain
  B Indians
  C buffalo
  D lightning

9 Nobody can get to Will to see if he is all right, because he is

  A lost on the river
  B stuck on a sandbar
  C riding through the storm
  D busy herding cattle across the river

10 The sight of a buffalo stampede makes Rachel

  A wish she could run after them
  B hide in the back of the wagon
  C cover her face with her bonnet
  D help drive the cattle farther away

Mark Student Reading Level:
___ Independent ___ Instructional ___ Listening

STOP

Comprehension

Grade 5, Unit 5: Under Western Skies

Name _____   Date _____

Lesson 24
WEEKLY TESTS 24.6

Simple Prefixes

Rachel's Journal
Decoding

*D*irections
Use what you know about simple prefixes to answer questions 1–10.
For each question, circle the letter next to your answer choice.

1 What is the base word of the word "mislead"?

   A mis
   B slead
   C lead
   D ead

2 What is the base word of the word "dishonest"?

   A dish
   B hone
   C honest
   D dishone

3 What is the base word of the word "insecure"?

   A secure
   B insec
   C cure
   D in

4 What is the base word of the word "disorder"?

   A diso
   B der
   C order
   D dis

5 What is the base word of the word "unlikely"?

   A like
   B unlike
   C ikley
   D un

6 What is the prefix of the word "incomplete"?

   A in
   B com
   C plete
   D incom

7 What is the prefix of the word "disaster"?

   A aster
   B disa
   C dis
   D er

8 What is the prefix of the word "dislikes"?

   A dislike
   B likes
   C dis
   D isli

Go On

Decoding
© Houghton Mifflin Harcourt Publishing Company. All rights reserved.

Grade 5, Unit 5: Under Western Skies

Name _____ Date _____

Lesson 24
WEEKLY TESTS 24.7

Rachel's Journal
Decoding

9 What is the prefix of the word "unequal"?

- **A** eq
- **B** une
- **C** qual
- **D** un

10 What is the prefix of the word "invisible"?

- **A** in
- **B** vis
- **C** ible
- **D** invis

STOP

Decoding

Grade 5, Unit 5: Under Western Skies

Lesson 24
WEEKLY TESTS 24.8

Name _____ Date _____

Making Comparisons

Rachel's Journal
Language Arts

*D*irections
Use what you know about making comparisons to answer questions 1–10. For each question, circle the letter next to your answer choice.

1 Which word or words **best** complete the sentence below?

> I did not know that Jason is _____ than Anna.

A taller
B tallest
C more taller
D most tall

2 Which word or words **best** complete the sentence below?

> Max is the _____ mule of all on the farm.

A stronger
B strongest
C more strong
D most strong

3 Which word or words **best** complete the sentence below?

> The sky looked _____ than it had earlier in the day.

A threateninger
B threateningest
C more threatening
D most threatening

4 Which word or words **best** complete the sentence below?

> I am five years _____ than Anthony.

A younger
B youngest
C more younger
D most youngest

Go On

Language Arts
© Houghton Mifflin Harcourt Publishing Company. All rights reserved.

Grade 5, Unit 5: Under Western Skies

Name _____ Date _____

Lesson 24
WEEKLY TESTS 24.9

Rachel's Journal
Language Arts

5 Which word or words **best** complete the sentence below?

> Keri is the _____ person in the world.

A happier
B happiest
C more happy
D most happiest

6 Which word or words **best** complete the sentence below?

> The tall clown is _____ than the short clown.

A funnier
B funniest
C more funnier
D most funny

7 Which word or words **best** complete the sentence below?

> Jessica had a cold and felt _____ as the day progressed.

A miserabler
B miserablest
C more miserable
D most miserable

8 Which word or words **best** complete the sentence below?

> Tommy had a _____ time feeding the ducks than feeding the geese.

A good
B better
C worser
D worst

9 Which word or words **best** complete the sentence below?

> The model car was priced _____ than the model airplane.

A reasonabler
B reasonablest
C more reasonably
D most reasonably

10 Which word or words **best** complete the sentence below?

> Last year we had the _____ blizzard our state has ever had.

A bad
B worse
C worst
D worstest

STOP

Language Arts
© Houghton Mifflin Harcourt Publishing Company. All rights reserved.

Grade 5, Unit 5: Under Western Skies

Name _____ Date _____

Lesson 25
WEEKLY TESTS 25.1

Lewis and Clark
Test Record Form

TEST RECORD FORM	Possible Score	Criterion Score	Student Score
Vocabulary: Target Vocabulary, Analogies	10	8	
Comprehension: Author's Purpose, Selection Test	10	8	
Decoding: Consonant Alternations	10	8	
Language Arts: Proper Mechanics	10	8	
TOTAL	40	32	

Total Student Score × 2.5 = _____ %

Go On

Test Record Form
© Houghton Mifflin Harcourt Publishing Company. All rights reserved.

Grade 5, Unit 5: Under Western Skies

Name _____ **Date** _____

Target Vocabulary, Analogies

Lesson 25
WEEKLY TESTS 25.2

Lewis and Clark
Vocabulary

*D*irections
Use what you know about the target vocabulary and analogies to answer questions 1–10. For each question, circle the letter next to your answer choice.

1 What does the word "range" mean in the sentence below?

The cattle grazed on the range.

A a star in the night sky
B a large area of open land
C a tool for measuring distance
D an original entrance to a building

2 What does the word "barrier" mean in the sentence below?

Quentin built a barrier around the garden.

A something that is bought at a store
B something that is used to dig holes
C something that is described in detail
D something that keeps out unwanted things

3 What does the word "expedition" mean in the sentence below?

The explorers went on an expedition to learn more about North America.

A journey
B caravan
C vacation
D short trip

4 What does the word "edible" mean in the sentence below?

In science class, we learned about some edible wild plants.

A fit to eat
B hard to find
C easy to grow
D pretty to look at

Vocabulary
© Houghton Mifflin Harcourt Publishing Company. All rights reserved.

Grade 5, Unit 5: Under Western Skies

Lesson 25
WEEKLY TESTS 25.3

Name _____ Date _____

Lewis and Clark
Vocabulary

5 What does the word "resumed" mean in the sentence below?

> Nora took a break and then resumed studying for her math test.

A read over
B began again
C worked quietly
D stopped completely

Use what you know about analogies to complete the analogies in questions 6–10.

6 *Glove* is to *hand* as *boot* is to

A arm
B face
C foot
D ankle

7 *Breakfast* is to *lunch* as *morning* is to

A sunrise
B midnight
C weekend
D afternoon

8 *Small* is to *tiny* as *large* is to

A huge
B short
C wide
D light

9 *Ear* is to *hear* as *mouth* is to

A feel
B taste
C listen
D smell

10 *Soap* is to *clean* as *mud* is to

A dirty
B earth
C rocks
D water

STOP

Vocabulary

Grade 5, Unit 5: Under Western Skies

Name _____ Date _____

Lesson 25
WEEKLY TESTS 25.4

Lewis and Clark
Comprehension

Author's Purpose, Selection Test

*D*irections
Think back to the selection "Lewis and Clark" to answer questions 1–10. For each question, circle the letter next to your answer choice.

1 Why does the author describe the sight of the Rocky Mountains as "inspiring as well as troubling"?

A The mountains would be difficult to cross.
B William Clark was afraid of heights.
C The men might easily get lost in the mountains.
D The view was sometimes hidden in fog.

2 Why does the author believe that Sacagawea's knowledge of local roots and fruit is important to the explorers?

A She saves them from starvation.
B She keeps them from eating poison food.
C She cooks and serves the men all their meals.
D She helps add variety and flavor to the meals.

3 The author believes that Lewis and Clark are

A on a journey that is not well-planned
B completely dependent upon Sacagawea
C confused often and irritated with each other
D competent men who accomplish something important

4 The author gets some of the information in the selection from

A Clark's writings only
B both men's writings
C Lewis's writings only
D neither man's writings

5 What is the author's purpose in writing this selection?

A to inform
B to entertain
C to convince
D to persuade

Comprehension
© Houghton Mifflin Harcourt Publishing Company. All rights reserved.

Grade 5, Unit 5: Under Western Skies

Lesson 25
WEEKLY TESTS 25.5

Name _____ Date _____

Lewis and Clark
Comprehension

6 The author **most likely** quotes from Lewis and Clark to show

A that he has researched the topic
B the real voices of the expedition leaders
C the different writing styles of the two men
D how important it is for everyone to keep a journal

7 How does the author **most likely** feel about the reunion between Sacagawea and Cameahwait?

A He doubts that the reunion took place.
B He thinks the reunion is humorous.
C He is suspicious of Cameahwait.
D He admires their display of emotions.

8 What does the author think of Sacagawea's contribution to the expedition?

A It is exaggerated, but still very important.
B It is a significant contribution in many ways.
C It is limited to the small act of pointing out landmarks.
D It is the most important element of the expedition's success.

9 What do the author's comments about the Nez Perce and the Chinook show?

A The Nez Perce and the Chinook were enemies.
B The Nez Perce and the Chinook were friends.
C The Nez Perce felt friendlier toward the explorers.
D The Chinook had less experience as traders.

10 According to the author, how did Thomas Jefferson feel about Lewis and Clark's achievement?

A He was disappointed that they didn't find an inland waterway.
B He was annoyed by how long it took for them to return.
C He was delighted with their many discoveries.
D He was jealous of their many adventures.

Mark Student Reading Level:
____ Independent ____ Instructional ____ Listening

STOP

Comprehension
© Houghton Mifflin Harcourt Publishing Company. All rights reserved.

Grade 5, Unit 5: Under Western Skies

Name _____ Date _____

Lesson 25
WEEKLY TESTS 25.6

Consonant Alternations

Lewis and Clark
Decoding

*D*irections
Use what you know about consonant alternations to answer questions 1–10. For each question, circle the letter next to your answer choice.

1 The word "elect" has the same sound for t as

  A vacation
  B elastic
  C option
  D catch

2 The word "election" has the same sound for t as

  A present
  B direction
  C return
  D travel

3 The word "express" has the same sound for s as

  A mission
  B measure
  C select
  D sure

4 The word "expression" has the same sound for s as

  A lease
  B select
  C handsome
  D insure

5 The word "sign" has the same sound for g as

  A begin
  B grand
  C light
  D legend

6 The word "signal" has the same sound for g as

  A right
  B guest
  C weight
  D judge

Decoding
© Houghton Mifflin Harcourt Publishing Company. All rights reserved.

Grade 5, Unit 5: Under Western Skies

Name _____ Date _____

Lesson 25
WEEKLY TESTS 25.7

Lewis and Clark
Decoding

7 The word "celebrate" has the same sound for t as

   A departure
   B relation
   C fifteen
   D direction

8 The word "celebration" has the same sound for t as

   A depart
   B motion
   C sculpt
   D carton

9 The word "electric" has the same sound for c as

   A twice
   B recall
   C magician
   D decide

10 The word "politician" has the same sound for c as

   A recite
   B vacate
   C musician
   D school

STOP

Decoding
© Houghton Mifflin Harcourt Publishing Company. All rights reserved.

Grade 5, Unit 5: Under Western Skies

Name _____ Date _____

Lesson 25
WEEKLY TESTS 25.8

Proper Mechanics

Lewis and Clark
Language Arts

*D*irections
Use what you know about proper mechanics to answer questions 1–10. For each question, circle the letter next to your answer choice.

1 Which sentence is written correctly?

  A This summer I read a book entitled Camping Across America.
  B This summer I read a book entitled Camping Across America.
  C This summer I read a book entitled *camping across America.*
  D This summer I read a book entitled "Camping Across America."

2 Which sentence is written correctly?

  A That is *the best apple* I have ever eaten!
  B That is the best apple I have ever eaten!
  C That is the "best" apple I have ever eaten!
  D That is the "best apple" I have ever eaten!

3 Which sentence is written correctly?

  A Land of the midnight sun is the best movie Geri has ever seen.
  B *Land of the Midnight Sun* is the best movie Geri has ever seen.
  C *Land of the Midnight Sun* is the best movie Geri has ever seen.
  D "Land of the Midnight Sun" is the best movie Geri has ever seen.

4 Which sentence is written correctly?

  A The choir sang the song "Laugh, Laugh, Laugh" at the concert.
  B The choir sang the song Laugh, Laugh, Laugh at the concert.
  C The choir sang the song *Laugh, Laugh, Laugh* at the concert.
  D The choir sang the song laugh, laugh, "Laugh" at the concert.

Language Arts
© Houghton Mifflin Harcourt Publishing Company. All rights reserved.

Grade 5, Unit 5: Under Western Skies

Name _____   **Date** _____

Lesson 25
WEEKLY TESTS 25.9

Lewis and Clark
Language Arts

5 Which sentence is written correctly?

A Have you read the poem called autumn leaves?
B Have you read the poem called *Autumn Leaves*?
C Have you read the poem called "autumn leaves"?
D Have you read the poem called "Autumn Leaves"?

6 Which sentence is written correctly?

A The story, The Friendly Dinosaur, was written in 2001.
B The story, *The Friendly Dinosaur*, was written in 2001.
C The story, The Friendly "Dinosaur," was written in 2001.
D The story, "The Friendly Dinosaur," was written in 2001.

7 Which sentence is written correctly?

A How to Make a Kite is a story that tells the steps to follow to make a kite.
B "How to Make a Kite" is a story that tells the steps to follow to make a kite.
C *How to Make a Kite* is a story that tells the steps to follow to make a kite.
D How to make a "kite" is a story that tells the steps to follow to make a kite.

8 Which sentence is written correctly?

A Our class performed the play entitled, "The Life and Times of a Fifth Grader."
B Our class performed the play entitled, *The Life and Times of a Fifth Grader*.
C Our class performed the play entitled, The Life and Times of a fifth grader.
D Our class performed the play entitled, the life and times of a "Fifth Grader."

Go On

Language Arts
© Houghton Mifflin Harcourt Publishing Company. All rights reserved.

Grade 5, Unit 5: Under Western Skies

Lesson 25
WEEKLY TESTS 25.10

Name _____ Date _____

Lewis and Clark
Language Arts

9 Which sentence is written correctly?

  A Have you seen the movie *welcome home*?

  B Have you seen the movie *Welcome Home*?

  C Have you seen the movie "welcome Home"?

  D Have you seen the movie "Welcome Home"?

10 Which sentence is written correctly?

  A Martha read the story ten tiny toads to her little brother.

  B Martha read the story Ten Tiny Toads to her little brother.

  C Martha read the story *Ten Tiny Toads* to her little brother.

  D Martha read the story "Ten Tiny Toads" to her little brother.

STOP

Name _____ Date _____

Lesson 26
WEEKLY TESTS 26.1

Animals on the Move
Test Record Form

TEST RECORD FORM	Possible Score	Criterion Score	Student Score
Vocabulary: Target Vocabulary, Multiple-Meaning Words	10	8	
Comprehension: Text and Graphic Features, Selection Test	10	8	
Decoding: Prefixes and Word Roots	10	8	
Language Arts: Possessive Nouns	10	8	
TOTAL	40	32	

Total Student Score × 2.5 = _____ %

Test Record Form
© Houghton Mifflin Harcourt Publishing Company. All rights reserved.

Grade 5, Unit 6: Journey to Discovery

Lesson 26
WEEKLY TESTS 26.2

Name _____ Date _____

Animals on the Move
Vocabulary

Target Vocabulary, Multiple-Meaning Words

*D*irections
Use what you know about the target vocabulary and multiple-meaning words to answer questions 1–10. For each question, circle the letter next to your answer choice.

1 What does the word "disturbing" mean in the sentence below?

> Mandy watched the baby birds without disturbing the nest.

A seeing
B building
C rejecting
D bothering

2 What does the word "struggled" mean in the sentence below?

> Oscar struggled to carry the heavy package to his house.

A asked a friend
B created a machine
C used a lot of energy
D moved things around

3 What does the word "gradually" mean in the sentence below?

> The bus gradually came to a stop.

A recently
B properly
C little by little
D with some noise

4 What does the word "identical" mean in the sentence below?

> No two snowflakes are identical.

A exactly alike
B very unusual
C almost frozen
D simply elegant

Go On

Lesson 26
WEEKLY TESTS 26.3

Animals on the Move
Vocabulary

5 What does the word "routine" mean in the sentence below?

Every afternoon, Steven walked his dog as part of his routine.

A a humorous event
B a special ceremony
C a lesson that was learned
D a regular course of action

6 What does the word "blank" mean in the sentence below?

The coach had a blank look on his face.

A not written on
B without expression
C center spot of a target
D mark where a word was left out

7 What does the word "double" mean in the sentence below?

The price of a train ticket will double next month.

A a fold
B a twin
C have two layers
D be twice as much

8 What does the word "flip" mean in the sentence below?

We like to watch Mom flip the pancakes.

A to look quickly
B to snap something
C to turn over in the air
D to leaf through pages in a book

9 What does the word "check" mean in the sentence below?

The woman wrote a check to pay for her groceries.

A an inspection
B a sudden stop
C a ticket showing ownership
D a written order given to a bank

10 What does the word "rough" mean in the sentence below?

The road up the mountain was rough.

A a person that is rude
B a job that is done quickly
C a coat of hair that is shaggy
D a place that is hard to travel on

STOP

Vocabulary

Name _____ Date _____

Lesson 26
WEEKLY TESTS 26.4

Text and Graphic Features, Selection Test

Animals on the Move
Comprehension

*D*irections

Think back to the selection "Animals on the Move" to answer questions 1–10. For each question, circle the letter next to your answer choice.

1 Which quote from the selection **best** supports the title?

   A But traveling a long distance or an unknown route takes more planning.
   B Echoes are created when sound waves move through the air, hit something, and bounce back.
   C She listened to the tapes at normal speed and heard elephant sounds no human had ever heard before.
   D To navigate, they use these senses and other abilities that people don't have, such as echolocation, in ways that scientists are still trying to understand.

2 The section of the selection with the heading "Leaving Home" tells how

   A animals use infrasound
   B an animal will live its life
   C an animal uses echolocation
   D animals know how to communicate

3 The photograph on page 7 shows how elephants

   A move around in groups
   B use infrasound to find each other
   C all flap their ears at the same time
   D make low sounds to call their family

4 What do you learn by reading the text under the heading "Why Bees Sing and Dance"?

   A That animals have five senses
   B How some animals greet each other
   C That sound waves bounce off objects as an echo
   D How some animals tell others where to find food

Go On

Comprehension
© Houghton Mifflin Harcourt Publishing Company. All rights reserved.

Grade 5, Unit 6: Journey to Discovery

Lesson 26
WEEKLY TESTS 26.5

Animals on the Move
Comprehension

Name _____ Date _____

5 To find information about how some animals communicate with each other, you could look under any of these headings except

A "Elephant Talk"
B "Leaving Home"
C "Why Bats Squeak"
D "Why Bees Sing and Dance"

6 Which is the **best** place to find information about why scientists band animals' legs?

A text
B caption
C heading
D photograph

7 The **best** place in the selection to find information about tracking birds is in

A the title
B the text
C a heading
D a photograph

8 Which caption of a photograph tells about an animal learning from humans?

A *A crane in flight*
B *A honeybee's circular dance means flowers are nearby.*
C *Each year, thousands of salmon return to the waters where they hatched.*
D *Endangered whooping cranes learn a migration route by following an ultralight aircraft.*

9 The purpose of the photograph on page 12 is to show how geese

A follow a river
B fly in formation
C memorize their route
D use the sun as a compass

10 To find out how salmon find their way back to their birthplace, you would look under the heading

A "Elephant Talk"
B "Leaving Home"
C "Returning Home"
D "Why Bees Sing and Dance"

Mark Student Reading Level:
___ Independent   ___ Instructional   ___ Listening

STOP

Comprehension
© Houghton Mifflin Harcourt Publishing Company. All rights reserved.

Grade 5, Unit 6: Journey to Discovery

Lesson 26
WEEKLY TESTS 26.6

Name _____ Date _____

Animals on the Move
Decoding

Prefixes and Word Roots

*D*irections
Use what you know about prefixes and word roots to answer questions 1–10. For each question, circle the letter next to your answer choice.

1 Which word correctly completes the sentence below?

> My class took a trip to the wildlife _____.

A preserv
B perserve
C preserve
D proserve

2 Which word correctly completes the sentence below?

> Mom expressed _____ about the cold weather damaging her roses.

A cuncern
B consern
C concern
D comcern

3 Which word correctly completes the sentence below?

> Doug will _____ the square in a circle.

A incloes
B enclose
C emclose
D imclothes

4 Which word correctly completes the sentence below?

> The used bicycle was still in good _____.

A condition
B cundition
C condision
D condishun

Go On

Decoding
© Houghton Mifflin Harcourt Publishing Company. All rights reserved.

Grade 5, Unit 6: Journey to Discovery

Name _____ Date _____

Lesson 26
WEEKLY TESTS 26.7

Animals on the Move
Decoding

5 Which word correctly completes the sentence below?

> Cora had to _____ her new shirt because she bought the wrong size.

A exchang
B ixchange
C exchange
D ekschainge

6 Which word correctly completes the sentence below?

> Our teacher will _____ to read aloud the exciting story.

A continue
B continew
C comtinue
D comtinew

7 Which word correctly completes the sentence below?

> Some people in our city decided to _____ the new law.

A pertest
B portest
C pretest
D protest

8 Which word correctly completes the sentence below?

> I learned how to _____ a new vocabulary word.

A pernunce
B prenonce
C pronounce
D pernownce

9 Which word correctly completes the sentence below?

> The clerks at the store decided to have a _____ to see who could sell the most books.

A cotest
B cortist
C contest
D comtest

10 Which word correctly completes the sentence below?

> Do you know what _____ this rock serves?

A purpose
B preporse
C purpoise
D porpoise

STOP

Decoding
© Houghton Mifflin Harcourt Publishing Company. All rights reserved.

Grade 5, Unit 6: Journey to Discovery

Lesson 26
WEEKLY TESTS 26.8

Name _____ Date _____

Possessive Nouns

Animals on the Move
Language Arts

Directions
Use what you know about possessive nouns to answer questions 1–10. For each question, circle the letter next to your answer choice.

1 Which word correctly completes the sentence below?

My aunt belongs to the _____ club in her town.

A womans
B womans'
C women's
D womens'

2 Which word correctly completes the sentence below?

The _____ department is at the front of the store.

A child's
B children's
C childrens'
D childrene's

3 Which word correctly completes the sentence below?

Our _____ names are Ms. Henderson and Ms. Lee.

A coach
B coach's
C coache's
D coaches'

4 Which word correctly completes the sentence below?

The _____ top skier is coming to speak to us.

A country's
B countrys'
C countries
D countrie's

5 Which word correctly completes the sentence below?

The _____ race has 300 runners in it.

A mans
B mans'
C men's
D mens'

6 Which word correctly completes the sentence below?

Our _____ employees have volunteered to clean up the park.

A citie's
B cities'
C citys'
D city's

Go On

Language Arts
© Houghton Mifflin Harcourt Publishing Company. All rights reserved.

Grade 5, Unit 6: Journey to Discovery

Lesson 26
WEEKLY TESTS 26.9

Animals on the Move
Language Arts

Name _____ Date _____

7 Which word correctly completes the sentence below?

> Both _____ backpacks are on the desk.

A twins'
B twin's
C twins's
D twine's

8 Which word correctly completes the sentence below?

> This _____ goal is to raise money for a new hospital.

A communitys'
B community's
C communities
D communitie's

9 Which word correctly completes the sentence below?

> The principal liked the three _____ science fair projects.

A students
B students'
C student's
D studente's

10 Which word correctly completes the sentence below?

> One little _____ balloon floated into the clouds.

A girl's
B girls'
C girls's
D girle's

STOP

Language Arts
© Houghton Mifflin Harcourt Publishing Company. All rights reserved.

Grade 5, Unit 6: Journey to Discovery

Name _____ Date _____

Lesson 27
WEEKLY TESTS 27.1

Mysteries at Cliff Palace
Test Record Form

TEST RECORD FORM	Possible Score	Criterion Score	Student Score
Vocabulary: Target Vocabulary, Suffixes -ness, -less, -ment	10	8	
Comprehension: Theme, Selection Test	10	8	
Decoding: More Familiar Suffixes	10	8	
Language Arts: Abbreviations	10	8	
TOTAL	40	32	

Total Student Score × 2.5 = _____ %

Go On

Test Record Form
© Houghton Mifflin Harcourt Publishing Company. All rights reserved.

Grade 5, Unit 6: Journey to Discovery

Lesson 27
WEEKLY TESTS 27.2

Target Vocabulary, Suffixes -ness, -less, -ment

Mysteries at Cliff Palace
Vocabulary

*D*irections
Use what you know about the target vocabulary and suffixes -ness, -less, and -ment to answer questions 1–10. For each question, circle the letter next to your answer choice.

1 What does the word "stunned" mean in the sentence below?

> Caleb was stunned by the beauty of the waterfall.

A disgusted
B astonished
C challenged
D embarrassed

2 What does the word "analyzing" mean in the sentence below?

> After analyzing the problem, Jewel thought she found a solution.

A ignoring
B examining
C causing
D repeating

3 What does the word "resemble" mean in the sentence below?

> Some animals have patterns that resemble things in the environment.

A look like
B reflect on
C take apart
D grow from

4 What does the word "available" mean in the sentence below?

> The author will be available to speak to the class next Thursday.

A ready and willing
B intelligent and witty
C confused and unhappy
D prepared and entertaining

Vocabulary
© Houghton Mifflin Harcourt Publishing Company. All rights reserved.

Grade 5, Unit 6: Journey to Discovery

Name _____ Date _____

Lesson 27
WEEKLY TESTS 27.3

Mysteries at Cliff Palace
Vocabulary

5 What does the word "adapted" mean in the sentence below?

   Over time, the snake adapted so it could live in the desert.

   A failed
   B relaxed
   C changed
   D blundered

6 What does the word "achievement" mean in the sentence below?

   Tara won an award for her achievement in science.

   A quality work
   B cooperative effort
   C detailed instruction
   D unusual experiments

7 What does the word "equipment" mean in the sentence below?

   The farmer needed new equipment to harvest the crops.

   A food used for plants
   B boards used for fences
   C things needed for a task
   D sunlight needed for energy

8 What does the word "kindness" mean in the sentence below?

   The girl showed the frog kindness by carrying it to the pond.

   A never kind
   B being kind again
   C a person who is kind
   D the act of being kind

9 What does the word "worthless" mean in the sentence below?

   The rock Sheila found turned out to be worthless.

   A full of worth
   B without worth
   C one that has worth
   D before having worth

10 What does the word "darkness" mean in the sentence below?

   Pedro could not see in the darkness when the electricity went out.

   A without light
   B without grace
   C without charm
   D without reason

STOP

Vocabulary

Grade 5, Unit 6: Journey to Discovery

© Houghton Mifflin Harcourt Publishing Company. All rights reserved.

Name _____ Date _____

Lesson 27
WEEKLY TESTS 27.4

Theme, Selection Test

Mysteries at Cliff Palace
Comprehension

Directions
Think back to the selection "Mysteries at Cliff Palace" to answer questions 1–10. For each question, circle the letter next to your answer choice.

1 Ruben thinks that when he sees Cliff Palace up close, he will

   A find his missing notebook
   B learn why the Puebloans disappeared
   C use his lucky pen to draw a picture of the dwellings
   D climb into the sandstone alcoves in the cliff dwellings

2 Rosa thinks that Ruben will

   A find his lucky pen
   B fail to solve any mystery
   C learn how to make sandstone bricks
   D discover what happened to the Puebloans

3 The Spanish word "verde" means

   A tree
   B table
   C plant
   D green

4 The alcoves in the cliff dwellings were caused by

   A people digging them out
   B crumbling and breaking sandstone
   C towers that fell down through the years
   D water rushing through the cliff dwellings

5 A kiva is a

   A room
   B tower
   C plateau
   D canyon

6 What is the **most likely** reason the Ancestral Puebloans built their homes in the side of a cliff?

   A to store food for times of drought
   B to catch rainwater as it flowed down the cliff
   C to protect themselves from being attacked by others
   D to make sure they had a good place to live for generations

Comprehension
© Houghton Mifflin Harcourt Publishing Company. All rights reserved.

Grade 5, Unit 6: Journey to Discovery

Name _____ Date _____

Lesson 27
WEEKLY TESTS 27.5

Mysteries at Cliff Palace
Comprehension

7 All of these are reasons why the Ancestral Puebloans may have left the Mesa Verde area except

   A other people kept stealing their food
   B they had to fight others for good land
   C it became too dry for them to grow food
   D another group of people moved into Cliff Palace

Detail: Ruben cannot find his lucky pen or his notebook.	Detail: Ruben tries to figure out why the Pueblo people left Mesa Verde.	Detail:
↓	↓	↓

Theme: Some mysteries in life can be solved, and others cannot.

8 Who discovers Ruben's missing pen?

   A Dad
   B Mom
   C Rosa
   D Ruben

10 Which of these completes the graphic organizer?

   A Ruben finds his lost items.
   B Ruben researches how the Cliff Palace was built.
   C Ruben tells Rosa there was drought at Mesa Verde.
   D Ruben learns that the Puebloans moved away because of a war.

9 What happens to Ruben's lucky pen?

   A Dad borrows it.
   B Mom picks it up.
   C Rosa hides it from him.
   D Ranger Jenkins loses it.

Mark Student Reading Level:
____ Independent   ____ Instructional   ____ Listening

STOP

Comprehension
© Houghton Mifflin Harcourt Publishing Company. All rights reserved.

Grade 5, Unit 6: Journey to Discovery

Name _____ Date _____

Lesson 27
WEEKLY TESTS 27.6

More Familiar Suffixes

Mysteries at Cliff Palace
Decoding

Directions
Use what you know about suffixes to answer questions 1–10. For each question, circle the letter next to your answer choice.

1 Which word correctly completes the sentence below?

> The _____ sold her goods at the market in town.

A merchist
B merchent
C merchant
D merchable

2 Which word correctly completes the sentence below?

> The police officer showed great _____ during the earthquake.

A heroist
B heroism
C heroible
D heroable

3 Which word correctly completes the sentence below?

> The _____ hung his paintings at the museum.

A artist
B artent
C artism
D artable

4 Which word correctly completes the sentence below?

> Gerard had a _____ day at the beach.

A pleasent
B pleasant
C pleasible
D pleasable

Decoding
© Houghton Mifflin Harcourt Publishing Company. All rights reserved.

Grade 5, Unit 6: Journey to Discovery

Name _____ Date _____

Lesson 27
WEEKLY TESTS 27.7

Mysteries at Cliff Palace
Decoding

5 Which word correctly completes the sentence below?

> The chief gave the secret _____ her assignment.

A agist
B agant
C agent
D agism

6 Which word correctly completes the sentence below?

> The teacher thanked his students for doing a _____ job on the scenery for the play.

A remarkant
B remarkent
C remarkible
D remarkable

7 Which word correctly completes the sentence below?

> Sally wrote a note using _____ ink.

A invisent
B invisant
C invisible
D invisable

8 Which word correctly completes the sentence below?

> My niece wants to be a _____ when she grows up.

A scientist
B scientent
C scientant
D scientism

9 Which word correctly completes the sentence below?

> Dad wanted to be sure he paid a _____ price for Joanne's new bicycle.

A reasonist
B reasonism
C reasonible
D reasonable

10 Which word correctly completes the sentence below?

> Kelly went home from work with a _____ cold.

A horrist
B horrism
C horrible
D horrable

STOP

Decoding
© Houghton Mifflin Harcourt Publishing Company. All rights reserved.

Grade 5, Unit 6: Journey to Discovery

Name _____ Date _____

Lesson 27
WEEKLY TESTS 27.8

Abbreviations

Mysteries at Cliff Palace
Language Arts

Directions
Use what you know about abbreviations to answer questions 1–10. For each question, circle the letter next to your answer choice.

1 Which phrase correctly completes the sentence below?

_____ prepared for the meeting.

A Ms Alice n Hawes
B Ms Alice N. Hawes
C Ms. Alice N Hawes
D Ms. Alice N. Hawes

2 Which phrase correctly completes the sentence below?

We mailed the package to _____.

A 16 Pumpkin st in Little Elm, tx
B 16 Pumpkin Str in Little Elm, tx
C 16 Pumpkin St. in Little Elm, TX
D 16 Pumpkin ST. in Little Elm, Tx

3 Which phrase correctly completes the sentence below?

_____, is my dad's full name.

A Dr. Thomas J. Lang, Jr.
B Dtr. Thomas j. Lang, JR
C Doc. Thomas J Lang, jr.
D Dc. Thomas J. Lang, Jnr.

4 Which phrase correctly completes the sentence below?

Our grandparents are coming to visit on _____.

A Tues, dec. 15
B Tues., Dec. 15
C tsdy., decem. 15
D Tues., Dcmbr. 15

Language Arts
© Houghton Mifflin Harcourt Publishing Company. All rights reserved.

Grade 5, Unit 6: Journey to Discovery

Lesson 27
WEEKLY TESTS 27.9

Mysteries at Cliff Palace
Language Arts

5 Which phrase correctly completes the sentence below?

_____ is a famous author.

A C S Lewis
B C. S. Lewis
C c. s. Lewis
D Cl. St. Lewis

6 Which phrase correctly completes the sentence below?

Yesterday the students learned the difference between _____ in math class.

A an in, a ft, and a yd
B an in., a ft., and a yd.
C an In., a Ft., and a Yd.
D an in., a ft, and a yd

7 Which phrase correctly completes the sentence below?

_____ Kelsey went to the coast for their vacation.

A dr. and ms.
B dctr and mrs
C Dr. and Mrs.
D Doc. and Mis.

8 Which phrase correctly completes the sentence below?

Jason has lived at the corner of _____ for five years.

A Grand ave. and Lakeside dr.
B Grand Ave. and Lakeside Dr.
C Grand avnu and Lakeside dri
D Grand Av and Lakeside Dv

9 Which phrase correctly completes the sentence below?

_____ is a volcano in Washington state.

A mt. st. Helens
B Mt. St. Helens
C Mnt. St. Helens
D Mount. Snt. Helens

10 Which phrase correctly completes the sentence below?

On _____, the Falcons have soccer practice.

A mon, wed, and fri
B mon., wed., and fri.
C Mon., Wed., and Fri.
D Mnd., Wds., and Frd.

STOP

Language Arts
Grade 5, Unit 6: Journey to Discovery

Name _____ Date _____

Lesson 28
WEEKLY TESTS 28.1

Fossils: A Peek into the Past
Test Record Form

TEST RECORD FORM	Possible Score	Criterion Score	Student Score
Skills in Context: Fact and Opinion, Target Vocabulary	10	8	
Vocabulary: Target Vocabulary, Idioms (Adages & Common Sayings)	10	8	
Comprehension: Fact and Opinion, Selection Test	10	8	
Decoding: Greek Word Roots	10	8	
Language Arts: Commas in Sentences	10	8	
TOTAL	50	40	
		Total Student Score × 2 =	%

Test Record Form
© Houghton Mifflin Harcourt Publishing Company. All rights reserved.

Grade 5, Unit 6: Journey to Discovery

Fact and Opinion, Target Vocabulary

Fossils: A Peek into the Past
Skills in Context

Directions Read the selection. Then read each question that follows the selection. Decide which is the best answer to each question. For each question, circle the letter next to your answer choice.

Museum of the West Digs into the Past

If you have driven out of town on Route 7 in the last several months, you have probably noticed people working on the cliffs above Roaring River. The people are researchers from the Museum of the West, and they have made some exciting discoveries about the area in which we live.

After months of carefully digging in a promising cliff, museum archaeologists found a huge collection of fossils. Museum director Sarah Wiggins says, "This is a tremendous find. There are fish fossils, pieces of Native American pottery, and even some whole animal skeletons. Obviously, a group of people must have lived in this spot near the river."

The cliffs by the river and those that roads have been cut through clearly show different layers. These are sedimentary rock, laid down layer by layer. Long ago, the land our city is built upon was covered by water. Pieces of earth and rock washed into the sea, animals died, and ancient people threw things into the sea. Everything sank to the bottom and was trapped in the layer that was forming at the time. Later, the sea dried up, and a river began to cut through the land. The power of the running water left the familiar terrain that surrounds our city.

Wiggins described the dig as the largest number of index fossils ever found in the area. She explained that an index fossil is one that can be used to tell the age of the land in which the fossil is found. She and her team will excavate the fossils and use them to determine how long ago each layer of sediment was laid down.

Head of Museum Research, Rick Fowler, explains how an organized dig works. "The cliff is marked off in numbered grids, using spikes and string," he says. "This way, we can keep track of where we find each fossil." They also take photographs of each fossil before it is carefully removed, bagged, and labeled by the location where it was found. Then the fossils are taken to the museum for research.

Go On

"Kids will love this," says Fowler. "We'll let the public know when the fossils will be on display. By then, we should know much more about them and the time frame of when they were formed. It will be fun and educational for every citizen of our town."

Wiggins adds, "We won't remove all the fossils. Many will be left behind. Right now, the area is fenced off so nobody but museum personnel can get to it. But later, when we are finished, our education director will create a training class for amateur archaeologists. Adults and children will be able to sign up to be part of a fossil dig."

This exciting news will most likely prompt many curious visitors to try to visit the site. The Museum of the West hopes to persuade people to stay away from the dig until it is open to the public.

Wiggins suggests that interested people contact the Roaring River Rock Club. That organization already has classes that teach beginning archaeology, and it leads field trips to other cliff areas around town, where students can dig for fossils.

In addition, the Rock Club has supplies and tools available to students so they can dig safely. Most individuals will not want to provide their own shovels, picks, rock hammers, and other equipment. It is important to use correct tools and to learn proper scientific methods for finding and caring for fossils.

The Museum of the West will post information about the dig on its website. The weekly calendar in the *Roaring River Times* will let the public know when the display is ready. Citizens are encouraged to come by the museum anytime.

---

1 An **opinion** expressed by Sarah Wiggins is that

 A the dig is a tremendous find
 B some animal skeletons have become fossils
 C fossils can be used to tell the age of the land
 D the fossil-dig area is fenced off from the public

2 Which event happens **first**?

 A Water covers the land.
 B Rock is laid down layer by layer.
 C Fossils are photographed where they are found.
 D Cliffs are exposed by cutting roads through them.

Name _____ Date _____

Lesson 28
WEEKLY TESTS 28.4

Fossils: A Peek into the Past
Skills in Context

3 The cliffs around the town were exposed by

A index fossils
B running water
C sedimentary rock
D museum researchers

4 What does the word "organized" mean as used in the passage?

A valued
B planned
C equipped
D condensed

5 A **fact** stated in this selection is that

A kids will love the fossil display
B the article will attract curious visitors to the site
C people interested in a dig can call the Rock Club
D the display will be fun and educational for everyone

6 An **opinion** expressed in the selection is

A the cliffs show different layers of rock
B researchers have made exciting discoveries
C grids help keep track of where fossils are found
D museum personnel will not remove all the fossils

Go On

Skills in Context
© Houghton Mifflin Harcourt Publishing Company. All rights reserved.

Grade 5, Unit 6: Journey to Discovery

Name _____ Date _____

Lesson 28
WEEKLY TESTS 28.5

Fossils: A Peek into the Past
Skills in Context

7 It is a **fact** stated in the selection that

  A researchers carefully dug up a collection of fossils
  B town citizens have probably seen the work going on at the cliffs
  C researchers will be able to tell for sure when the fossils were formed
  D people can learn when the display is ready by reading the newspaper

8 What can the reader conclude after reading the selection?

  A The author is excited about the fossil find.
  B Kids and adults will call the Rock Club about classes.
  C People will put safety first when they try to find fossils.
  D The Rock Club will teach people how to cut through cliffs.

9 What does the word "persuade" mean as used in the passage?

  A to discuss
  B to operate
  C to convince
  D to appreciate

10 The author wrote this selection to

  A teach
  B inform
  C entertain
  D persuade

STOP

Lesson 28
WEEKLY TESTS 28.6

Name _____ Date _____

Target Vocabulary, Idioms (Adages & Common Sayings)

Fossils: A Peek into the Past
Vocabulary

Directions
Use what you know about the target vocabulary and idioms to answer questions 1–10. For each question, circle the letter next to your answer choice.

1 What does the word "viewpoint" mean in the sentence below?

> The candidate clearly stated her viewpoint.

A regret
B position
C comment
D education

2 What does the word "organize" mean in the sentence below?

> The fifth graders will organize a clean-up day for the school.

A plan
B view
C attend
D consider

3 What does the word "persuade" mean in the sentence below?

> In the story, the turtle tried to persuade the rabbit to have a race.

A ignore
B release
C astound
D convince

4 What does the word "rural" mean in the sentence below?

> My aunt and uncle moved away from the city so they could enjoy rural life.

A public
B diesel
C granite
D country

Go On

Name _____ Date _____

Lesson 28
WEEKLY TESTS 28.7

Fossils: A Peek into the Past
Vocabulary

5 What does the word "legendary" mean in the sentence below?

King Arthur was a legendary ruler.

A famous
B civilized
C intelligent
D enterprising

6 What does this sentence mean?

For Joel, the test was a piece of cake.

A Joel took the test after lunch.
B Joel thought the test was easy.
C Joel completed several sections on the test.
D Joel answered only a few questions on the test.

7 What does this sentence mean?

The highway workers decided to call it a day.

A The highway workers went home.
B The highway workers quit their jobs.
C The highway workers started a new road.
D The highway workers labored for many hours.

8 What does this sentence mean?

Danielle had to use elbow grease to clean her bicycle.

A Danielle had to ask for help to clean her bicycle.
B Danielle had to work hard to clean her bicycle.
C Danielle had to use chemicals to clean her bicycle.
D Danielle had to have more time to clean her bicycle.

Vocabulary

Grade 5, Unit 6: Journey to Discovery

Name _____ Date _____

Lesson 28
WEEKLY TESTS 28.8

Fossils: A Peek into the Past
Vocabulary

9 What does this sentence mean?

When Susan yawned, she knew it was time to hit the sack.

A When Susan yawned, she knew it was time to go to school.
B When Susan yawned, she knew it was time to clean her room.
C When Susan yawned, she knew it was time to go to bed.
D When Susan yawned, she knew it was time to stop reading.

10 What does this sentence mean?

Min knew that, if he did not step on it, he would miss the bus.

A Min knew that, if he did not hurry up, he would miss the bus.
B Min knew that, if he did not get up on time, he would miss the bus.
C Min knew that, if he did not check the schedule, he would miss the bus.
D Min knew that, if he did not watch where he was going, he would miss the bus.

STOP

- -

Vocabulary
© Houghton Mifflin Harcourt Publishing Company. All rights reserved.

Grade 5, Unit 6: Journey to Discovery

Name _____ Date _____

Lesson 28
WEEKLY TESTS 28.9

Fossils: A Peek into the Past
Comprehension

Fact and Opinion, Selection Test

Directions
Think back to the selection "Fossils: A Peek into the Past" to answer questions 1–10. For each question, circle the letter next to your answer choice.

1 Which phrase in the sentence "A ten-year-old boy named Jared Post had made a fantastic find" indicates that the statement is an **opinion**?

A *had made*
B *boy named*
C *ten-year-old*
D *fantastic find*

2 A **fact** expressed in the selection is that the rock Jared found

A was amazing
B had weird markings
C was a fossilized tooth
D created big news from Alaska

3 The section under the heading "Imagine a Woolly Mammoth!" states the **opinion** that woolly mammoths

A walked around Jared's neighborhood
B most likely used their tusks to scrape snow
C are thought to be related to today's elephants
D left fossils that tell us they once lived in certain areas

4 What is the author's **opinion** of woolly mammoths?

A They are fascinating.
B They ate plants for food.
C They only left behind their teeth as fossils.
D They are the only extinct mammals that left fossils.

5 Which heading expresses an **opinion**?

A "Traces of the Past"
B "Nature's Memory Keepers"
C "Imagine a Woolly Mammoth"
D "One Girl's Remarkable Finds"

6 You can tell that the author has the **opinion** that children who discover fossils

A will become scientists
B are interesting to learn about
C are smarter than other children
D know a lot about extinct animals

Comprehension
© Houghton Mifflin Harcourt Publishing Company. All rights reserved.

Grade 5, Unit 6: Journey to Discovery

Name _____ Date _____

Lesson 28
WEEKLY TESTS 28.10

Fossils: A Peek into the Past
Comprehension

7 What could prove that 2007 was "a great year for finds" is a **fact**?

A if Jared, Sierra, and Kaleb wrote a book about finding fossils in 2007
B if Mary agreed that 2007 was one of the great years for finding fossils
C if the fossils found in 2007 proved that woolly mammoths were still alive
D if the author compared the 2007 fossil finds to every other year's finds

8 The phrase that says fossils "help us understand what the world was like" is an **opinion** because it

A states a fact
B gives a clue
C defines a word
D expresses a belief

9 An **opinion** expressed in the selection is that Mary Anning

A was born in England
B found a fossil of a sea reptile
C was the greatest fossilist in the world
D discovered a fossil when she was eleven

10 Which statement from the selection expresses an **opinion**?

A *The Ice Age occurred between 1.6 million and 10,000 years ago.*
B *She discovered the skeleton of a giant sea creature when she was about eleven years old.*
C *Another super-successful young fossil hunter was Mary Anning, who was born on the south coast of England.*
D *Although mammoths roamed throughout much of North America, Europe, Asia, and Africa, their bones and teeth are found mainly in areas with very cold weather.*

Mark Student Reading Level:
____ Independent   ____ Instructional   ____ Listening

STOP

Comprehension
© Houghton Mifflin Harcourt Publishing Company. All rights reserved.

Grade 5, Unit 6: Journey to Discovery

Lesson 28
WEEKLY TESTS 28.11

Name _____ Date _____

Fossils: A Peek into the Past
Decoding

Greek Word Roots

*D*irections
Use what you know about Greek word roots to answer questions 1–10. For each question, circle the letter next to your answer choice.

1 What are the word parts in the word "telephoto"?

A   telep • hoto
B   tele • photo
C   teleph • oto
D   tel • ephoto

2 What are the word parts in the word "thermal"?

A   therm • al
B   ther • mal
C   the • rmal
D   th • ermal

3 What are the word parts in the word "biography"?

A   bi • ography
B   biog • raphy
C   bio • graphy
D   biograph • y

4 What are the word parts in the word "geology"?

A   geo • logy
B   geol • ogy
C   geolog • y
D   ge • ology

5 What are the word parts in the word "bicycle"?

A   bic • ycle
B   bi • cycle
C   bicy • cle
D   bicyc • le

6 Which word does NOT share a Greek root with the others?

A   Lag
B   Logo
C   Logic
D   Logical

Decoding
© Houghton Mifflin Harcourt Publishing Company. All rights reserved.

Grade 5, Unit 6: Journey to Discovery

Lesson 28
WEEKLY TESTS 28.12

Name _____ Date _____

Fossils: A Peek into the Past
Decoding

7 Which word does NOT share a Greek root with the others?

A decade
B declare
C decimal
D decimeter

8 Which word **best** completes the sentence below?

> Jeff says he wants to be an _____ and explore other planets.

A astronaut
B astronomy
C disaster
D asterisk

9 Which word **best** completes the sentence below?

> The _____ showed that it was colder outside than we thought.

A diameter
B barometer
C thermometer
D centimeter

10 Which word **best** completes the sentence below?

> The scientist studied the tiny bacteria through her _____.

A microscope
B microwave
C microcosm
D microphone

STOP

Decoding
© Houghton Mifflin Harcourt Publishing Company. All rights reserved.

Grade 5, Unit 6: Journey to Discovery

Name _____ Date _____

Commas in Sentences

Lesson 28
WEEKLY TESTS 28.13

Fossils: A Peek into the Past
Language Arts

Directions
Use what you know about commas in sentences to answer questions 1–10. For each question, circle the letter next to your answer choice.

1 Which sentence uses commas correctly?

   A Jason, what movie are your parents taking you to see?
   B Jason what movie, are your parents taking you to see?
   C Jason what movie, are your parents, taking you to see?
   D Jason, what movie, are your parents, taking you to see?

2 Which sentence uses commas correctly?

   A Suddenly there was a loud knock, at the door.
   B Suddenly there was, a loud knock at the door.
   C Suddenly, there was a loud knock at the door.
   D Suddenly, there was a loud knock, at the door.

3 Which sentence uses commas correctly?

   A No that is not, your notebook.
   B No, that is not your notebook.
   C No that is not your, notebook.
   D No, that is not, your notebook.

4 Which sentence uses commas correctly?

   A However, this will be the last time people can drive across the old bridge.
   B However this will be the last time, people can drive across the old bridge.
   C However, this will be, the last time people can drive across the old bridge.
   D However this will be the last time people can drive, across the old bridge.

5 Which sentence uses commas correctly?

   A Olivia, have you been to the store yet?
   B Olivia have you been to the store, yet?
   C Olivia, have you, been to the store yet?
   D Olivia have you, been to the store, yet?

Language Arts
© Houghton Mifflin Harcourt Publishing Company. All rights reserved.

Grade 5, Unit 6: Journey to Discovery

Lesson 28
WEEKLY TESTS 28.14

Name _____ Date _____

Fossils: A Peek into the Past
Language Arts

6 Which sentence uses commas correctly?

A Gloria can you fold the clean, clothes?
B Gloria, can you fold the clean clothes?
C Gloria can, you fold the clean clothes?
D Gloria, can you fold, the clean clothes?

7 Which sentence uses commas correctly?

A By the time Mom got home Dad, and I had already made dinner.
B By the time, Mom got home Dad and I had already made dinner.
C By the time Mom got home, Dad and I had already made dinner.
D By the time Mom got home, Dad, and I, had already made dinner.

8 Which sentence uses commas correctly?

A If Zach lost his ticket he will, need to buy a new one.
B If Zach lost his ticket, he will need to buy a new one.
C If Zach, lost his ticket he will need to buy a new one.
D If, Zach, lost his ticket, he will need to buy a new one.

9 Which sentence uses commas correctly?

A When it was morning the family began to prepare for, their trip.
B When it was morning the family began to prepare, for their trip.
C When it was morning, the family began, to prepare for their trip.
D When it was morning, the family began to prepare for their trip.

10 Which sentence uses commas correctly?

A Yes, we will have a picnic on Saturday if it does not rain.
B Yes we will have a picnic, on Saturday, if it does not rain.
C Yes, we will, have a picnic on Saturday if, it does not rain.
D Yes we will have, a picnic, on Saturday, if it does not rain.

STOP

Language Arts
Grade 5, Unit 6: Journey to Discovery

Name _____ Date _____

Lesson 29
WEEKLY TESTS 29.1

The Case of the Missing Deer
Test Record Form

TEST RECORD FORM	Possible Score	Criterion Score	Student Score
Vocabulary: Target Vocabulary, Greek and Latin Roots	10	8	
Comprehension: Conclusions and Generalizations, Selection Test	10	8	
Decoding: Latin Word Roots	10	8	
Language Arts: More Commas	10	8	
TOTAL	40	32	

Total Student Score × 2.5 = _____ %

Test Record Form
© Houghton Mifflin Harcourt Publishing Company. All rights reserved.

Grade 5, Unit 6: Journey to Discovery

Lesson 29
WEEKLY TESTS 29.2

Name _____ Date _____

Target Vocabulary, Greek and Latin Roots

The Case of the Missing Deer
Vocabulary

*D*irections
Use what you know about the target vocabulary and Greek and Latin roots to answer questions 1–10. For each question, circle the letter next to your answer choice.

1 What does the word "destination" mean in the sentence below?

> The destination for our field trip was an art museum.

A the things one is using
B the people one is meeting
C the time when one is living
D the place where one is going

2 What does the word "required" mean in the sentence below?

> The students are required to wear uniforms.

A demanded
B concerned
C challenged
D determined

3 What does the word "effective" mean in the sentence below?

> The new brakes on the electric car were effective.

A cost a lot
B broke down
C worked well
D squealed loudly

4 What does the word "dependent" mean in the sentence below?

> The dog is dependent on its owners for the care it receives.

A relying on
B targeting on
C trembling on
D reflecting on

Go On

Vocabulary
© Houghton Mifflin Harcourt Publishing Company. All rights reserved.

Grade 5, Unit 6: Journey to Discovery

Lesson 29
WEEKLY TESTS 29.3

Name _____ Date _____

The Case of the Missing Deer
Vocabulary

5 What does the word "suspense" mean in the sentence below?

> The adventure story was full of suspense.

A regret
B pleasure
C confidence
D uncertainty

6 What does the word "transported" mean in the sentence below?

> Imagine riding in a spaceship and being transported to another planet.

A carried
B flipped
C adapted
D launched

7 What does the word "interrupting" mean in the sentence below?

> The baby kept interrupting the conversation.

A breaking into
B describing for
C entertaining by
D comparing with

8 What does the word "telephone" mean in the sentence below?

> Mom will answer the telephone.

A a plant used to make medicine
B a chemical used to do an experiment
C a container used for storing information
D a machine used to speak to another person

9 What does the word "autographed" mean in the sentence below?

> The author autographed his new book.

A took his time
B wrote his name
C finished his job
D liked his review

10 What does the word "thermometer" mean in the sentence below?

> The thermometer showed that Orson had a fever.

A tool for measuring weight
B tool for measuring volume
C tool for measuring distance
D tool for measuring temperature

STOP

Vocabulary
Grade 5, Unit 6: Journey to Discovery

Name _____ Date _____

Lesson 29
WEEKLY TESTS 29.4

The Case of the Missing Deer
Comprehension

Conclusions and Generalizations, Selection Test

D*irections*
Think back to the selection "The Case of the Missing Deer" to answer questions 1–10. For each question, circle the letter next to your answer choice.

1 What conclusion can you draw from Grandpa's comment, "You'll have to wait until it cools off"?

  A Blake will burn his mouth if he eats dinner too soon.
  B They will have a campfire when the sun goes down.
  C It is too hot during the day for deer to come close to the cabins.
  D The other kids will come out to play soccer in the evening.

2 One of the **main** reasons Blake is excited about his family's vacation cabin is that

  A it is near three other cabins
  B it is hidden deep in the woods
  C he will have kids to play soccer with
  D he will have an unusual chance to see deer

3 You can tell that all four of the children

  A like to play soccer
  B go to school together
  C come to the cabins every year
  D put food out to attract the deer

4 What did Blake think was the reason why no deer showed up at his cabin the first night?

  A It was too cold outside.
  B He had not put out food.
  C The deer did not like his cabin.
  D There were no deer in the woods.

5 What can you infer about Blake?

  A He gets angry easily.
  B He wants to hunt deer.
  C He thinks his friends are lying.
  D He likes to find answers to questions.

6 Nicholas thinks that the reason the deer stay away from Blake's cabin could be

  A the sound of Blake's soccer ball
  B the lawn chairs and pinecones in the yard
  C that the deer like the people in the other cabins better
  D that the cabin is too far away from the edge of the woods

Go On

Comprehension
© Houghton Mifflin Harcourt Publishing Company. All rights reserved.

Grade 5, Unit 6: Journey to Discovery

Name _____ Date _____

Lesson 29
WEEKLY TESTS 29.5

The Case of the Missing Deer
Comprehension

7 When no deer come to his cabin, Blake **most likely** feels

A hesitant
B puzzled
C shunned
D impatient

8 Blake realizes why the deer have avoided his cabin when he

A sees uneaten apples
B reads a magazine article
C dribbles the soccer ball around pinecones
D sees deer tracks turning away from the cabin

9 Deer **most likely** try to avoid humans because

A people smell bad
B deer are cautious
C fawns are too curious
D deer like to stay hidden

10 What will **most likely** happen **next** in the story?

A Blake will stop looking for deer each night.
B The children will try to solve another mystery.
C Deer will show up at Blake's cabin more often.
D All the children will put out apples for the deer.

Mark Student Reading Level:
____ Independent   ____ Instructional   ____ Listening

STOP

Comprehension
Grade 5, Unit 6: Journey to Discovery

Name _____   Date _____

Latin Word Roots

Lesson 29
WEEKLY TESTS 29.6

The Case of the
Missing Deer
Decoding

*D*irections
Use what you know about Latin word roots to answer questions 1–10. For each question, circle the letter next to your answer choice.

1 What are the word parts in the word "transport"?

A trans • port
B tra • nsport
C transpo • rt
D transp • ort

2 What are the word parts in the word "spectator"?

A spectat • or
B spe • ctator
C spect • ator
D spectat • or

3 What are the word parts in the word "interrupt"?

A inter • rupt
B int • errupt
C interr • upt
D inte • rrupt

4 What are the word parts in the word "dictionary"?

A dict • ionary
B di • ctionary
C dic • tionary
D dicti • onary

5 What are the word parts in the word "construct"?

A con • struct
B constr • uct
C co • nstruct
D cons • truct

6 Which word does NOT share a Latin root with the others?

A love
B involve
C revolve
D evolve

7 Which word does NOT share a Latin root with the others?

A contradict
B verdict
C diction
D ditch

Go On

Decoding
© Houghton Mifflin Harcourt Publishing Company. All rights reserved.

Grade 5, Unit 6: Journey to Discovery

Name _____ **Date** _____

Lesson 29
WEEKLY TESTS 29.7

The Case of the Missing Deer
Decoding

8 Which word **best** completes the sentence below?

> The _____ said my teeth were clean and healthy.

A trident
B dental
C indent
D dentist

9 Which word **best** completes the sentence below?

> I tried to _____ the vase for any signs of damage.

A inspect
B respect
C spectacle
D spectral

10 Which word **best** completes the sentence below?

> Ships are used to _____ cargo across the ocean.

A ferry
B fertilize
C refer
D infer

STOP

Name _____ Date _____

Lesson 29
WEEKLY TESTS 29.8

More Commas

The Case of the
Missing Deer
Language Arts

Directions
Use what you know about commas to answer questions 1–10. For each question, circle the letter next to your answer choice.

1 Which sentence uses commas correctly?

A Pete our class president, has been absent a lot.
B Pete, our class president has been absent a lot.
C Pete, our class president, has been absent a lot.
D Pete, our class president has been, absent a lot.

2 Which sentence uses commas correctly?

A Leila the most talented writer, in our class, has written him a letter.
B Leila the most talented writer in our class, has written him a letter.
C Leila, the most talented writer in our class has written him a letter.
D Leila, the most talented writer in our class, has written him a letter.

3 Which sentence uses commas correctly?

A Darcy, the white dog with the black spots, is barking.
B Darcy the white dog, with the black spots, is barking.
C Darcy, the white dog, with the black spots, is barking.
D Darcy, the white, dog with the black, spots is barking.

4 Which sentence uses commas correctly?

A Celia, Rachel and I, live in Austin.
B Celia Rachel, and I live in Austin.
C Celia, Rachel, and I live in Austin.
D Celia, Rachel, and I, live in Austin.

Go On

Language Arts
© Houghton Mifflin Harcourt Publishing Company. All rights reserved.

Grade 5, Unit 6: Journey to Discovery

Lesson 29
WEEKLY TESTS 29.9

Name _____ Date _____

The Case of the Missing Deer
Language Arts

5 Which sentence uses commas correctly?

A On December 11 2005, we went to Washington D.C.
B On December 11 2005, we went to, Washington D.C.
C On December 11, 2005, we went to Washington, D.C.
D On December, 11 2005, we went to Washington, D.C.

6 Which sentence uses commas correctly?

A Polly, our parakeet with the yellow tail, is from New Mexico.
B Polly our parakeet, with the yellow tail, is from New Mexico.
C Polly, our parakeet, with the yellow tail is from New Mexico.
D Polly our parakeet with the yellow tail, is from, New Mexico.

7 Which sentence uses commas correctly?

A John Lenny and Peter, went to, the store.
B John, Lenny, and Peter went to the store.
C John, Lenny and Peter went, to the store.
D John, Lenny, and Peter, went to the store.

8 Which sentence uses commas correctly?

A The colors of our flag are red white, and blue.
B The colors of our flag are red, white, and blue.
C The colors, of our flag, are red white and blue.
D The colors of our flag, are red, white, and blue.

9 Which sentence uses commas correctly?

A We served pies cakes, cookies and candies.
B We served pies cakes cookies, and candies.
C We served pies, cakes cookies and candies.
D We served pies, cakes, cookies, and candies.

10 Which sentence uses commas correctly?

A I am going to Reno, Nevada on June 16.
B I am going to Reno Nevada, on June 16.
C I am going to, Reno Nevada, on June 16.
D I am going to Reno, Nevada, on June 16.

STOP

Language Arts
© Houghton Mifflin Harcourt Publishing Company. All rights reserved.

Grade 5, Unit 6: Journey to Discovery

Name _____ Date _____

Lesson 30
WEEKLY TESTS 30.1

**Get Lost!
The Puzzle of Mazes**
Test Record Form

TEST RECORD FORM	Possible Score	Criterion Score	Student Score
Vocabulary: Target Vocabulary, Word Origins	10	8	
Comprehension: Main Ideas and Details, Selection Test	10	8	
Decoding: Identifying VCV, VCCV, and VCCCV Syllable Patterns	10	8	
Language Arts: Other Punctuation	10	8	
TOTAL	40	32	

Total Student Score × 2.5 =   %

Go On

Test Record Form
© Houghton Mifflin Harcourt Publishing Company. All rights reserved.

Grade 5, Unit 6: Journey to Discovery

Lesson 30
WEEKLY TESTS 30.2

Name _____ Date _____

**Get Lost!
The Puzzle of Mazes**
Vocabulary

Target Vocabulary, Word Origins

*D*irections
Use what you know about the target vocabulary and word origins to answer questions 1–10. For each question, circle the letter next to your answer choice.

1 What does the word "pace" mean in the sentence below?

> The horse had to pick up his pace to jump over the fence.

A speed
B bridle
C license
D mission

2 What does the word "underestimated" mean in the sentence below?

> Billy underestimated how much paint he would need for the house.

A guessed too low
B poured too much
C mixed too quickly
D leaked too slowly

3 What does the word "residents" mean in the sentence below?

> The residents worked together to build a new playground for the children.

A people who live in a certain area
B people who work for the government
C people who travel from place to place
D people who volunteer to do helpful things

4 What does the word "techniques" mean in the sentence below?

> The teacher had many techniques for getting the students interested in learning.

A booths
B reasons
C methods
D instructions

Vocabulary
© Houghton Mifflin Harcourt Publishing Company. All rights reserved.

Grade 5, Unit 6: Journey to Discovery

Lesson 30
WEEKLY TESTS 30.3

Name _____ Date _____

**Get Lost!
The Puzzle of Mazes**
Vocabulary

5 What does the word "reasoned" mean in the sentence below?

> **The detective reasoned his way to solving the crime.**

A threw away
B jumped ahead
C became frustrated
D drew conclusions

6 Read the sentence below.

> **When the bell rings at the end of the day, Mr. Carson will dismiss the class.**

How does the word root miss help the reader understand what "dismiss" means?

A miss means "send"
B miss means "make"
C miss means "carry"
D miss means "break"

7 Read the sentence below.

> **The scientist used a telescope to see the stars and planets.**

How does the word root scop help the reader understand what "telescope" means?

A scop means "dig"
B scop means "see"
C scop means "earth"
D scop means "water"

8 Read the sentence below.

> **Julianne read a biography about Abraham Lincoln.**

How does the word root bio help the reader understand what "biography" means?

A bio means "fear"
B bio means "life"
C bio means "stone"
D bio means "word"

Go On

Vocabulary
© Houghton Mifflin Harcourt Publishing Company. All rights reserved.

Grade 5, Unit 6: Journey to Discovery

Name _____ Date _____

Lesson 30
WEEKLY TESTS 30.4

Get Lost!
The Puzzle of Mazes
Comprehension

9 Read the sentence below.

The farmer used his new tractor to plow his fields.

How does the word root tract help the reader understand what "tractor" means?

A tract means "step"
B tract means "take"
C tract means "pull"
D tract means "break"

10 Read the sentence below.

The captain of the ship gave the sailors their orders.

How does the word root cap help the reader understand what "captain" means?

A cap means "head"
B cap means "field"
C cap means "skill"
D cap means "place"

STOP

Vocabulary

Grade 5, Unit 6: Journey to Discovery

Main Ideas and Details, Selection Test

**Get Lost!
The Puzzle of Mazes**
Comprehension

Lesson 30
WEEKLY TESTS 30.5

Directions
Think back to the selection "Get Lost! The Puzzle of Mazes" to answer questions 1–10. For each question, circle the letter next to your answer choice.

1 What is the main idea of the first paragraph?

A Mazes are dangerous.
B Mazes are fascinating places.
C It is impossible to get out of a maze.
D You should carry a compass into a maze.

2 Read the diagram of information from the selection.

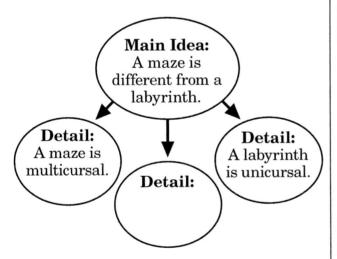

Which of these belongs in the empty circle?

A A maze is for children.
B A maze leads to a dead end.
C A labyrinth is made of hedges.
D A labyrinth may have no walls.

3 Yews make good hedges because they

A create all kinds of maze designs
B stay the same shape as they grow
C grow quickly to six feet or higher
D are easily trimmed into different shapes

4 What do all kinds of mazes have in common?

A Mazes have many paths.
B Maze paths end in the center.
C Maze paths go from side to side.
D Mazes are designs in a flat surface.

5 The Silver Jubilee maze is also known as the

A Turf Maze
B Leeds Castle Maze
C Longleat Hedge Maze
D aMazing Hedge Puzzle

Go On

Name _____ Date _____

Lesson 30
WEEKLY TESTS 30.6

**Get Lost!
The Puzzle of Mazes**
Comprehension

6 The creator of one of the longest mazes in the world is

A Greg Bright
B John Wayne
C Adrian Fisher
D Edward Heyes

7 Leeds Castle Maze contains all of the following features except

A a crown shape
B hedges made of corn
C an underground cave
D sculptures of animals

8 Which sentence **best** expresses the main idea of the section titled "Lost in the Cornstalks"?

A *Picture designs are especially popular for maize mazes.*
B *Our most common type of maze is made from cornstalks.*
C *It's nicknamed a maize maze because maize is another word for corn.*
D *Unlike hedge mazes, which last for years, maize mazes last for only one season.*

9 All of the following have been pictures in maize mazes except a

A map
B pyramid
C dinosaur
D cornstalk

10 Which character from Greek mythology has the head of a bull and the body of a man?

A Minos
B Ariadne
C Theseus
D Minotaur

Mark Student Reading Level:
____ Independent   ____ Instructional   ____ Listening

STOP

Comprehension

Grade 5, Unit 6: Journey to Discovery

Identifying VCV, VCCV, and VCCCV Syllable Patterns

Lesson 30
WEEKLY TESTS 30.7

Get Lost!
The Puzzle of Mazes
Decoding

Name _____ Date _____

Directions
Use what you know about syllable patterns to answer questions 1–10. For each question, circle the letter next to your answer choice.

1 What is the correct way to divide the word "dancer" into syllables?

  A danc • er
  B dan • cer
  C da • ncer
  D dance • r

2 What is the correct way to divide the word "cedar" into syllables?

  A ceda • r
  B c • edar
  C ced • ar
  D ce • dar

3 What is the correct way to divide the word "compliment" into syllables?

  A com • plim • ent
  B comp • li • ment
  C com • pli • ment
  D comp • lim • ent

4 What is the correct way to divide the word "ribbon" into syllables?

  A ribb • on
  B rib • bon
  C ri • bbon
  D ribbo • n

5 What is the correct way to divide the word "bouquet" into syllables?

  A bouq • uet
  B bou • quet
  C bo • uq • uet
  D bo • uqu • et

6 What is the correct way to divide the word "district" into syllables?

  A dis • trict
  B dist • rict
  C di • strict
  D distr • ict

Go On

Decoding
© Houghton Mifflin Harcourt Publishing Company. All rights reserved.

Grade 5, Unit 6: Journey to Discovery

Name _____ Date _____

Lesson 30
WEEKLY TESTS 30.8

**Get Lost!
The Puzzle of Mazes**
Decoding

7 What is the correct way to divide the word "letter" into syllables?

A l • etter
B le • tter
C lett • er
D let • ter

8 What is the correct way to divide the word "vacation" into syllables?

A vac • ati • on
B va • cat • ion
C va • ca • tion
D vac • at • ion

9 What is the correct way to divide the word "chorus" into syllables?

A cho • rus
B ch • orus
C chor • us
D choru • s

10 What is the correct way to divide the word "camel" into syllables?

A ca • mel
B cam • el
C came • l
D c • amel

STOP

Name _____ Date _____

Other Punctuation

Lesson 30
WEEKLY TESTS 30.9

Get Lost!
The Puzzle of Mazes
Language Arts

Directions
Use what you know about punctuation to answer questions 1–10.
For each question, circle the letter next to your answer choice.

1 Which sentence is written correctly?

  A Here are the supplies I need paper, (paint): different colors, paintbrushes, and water.
  B Here are the supplies I need: paper, paint (different colors), paintbrushes, and water.
  C Here are the: (supplies I need) paper, paint different colors, paintbrushes, and water.
  D Here are the supplies: I need (paper, paint different colors, paintbrushes, and water).

2 Which sentence is written correctly?

  A Corey finally admits (after taking time) to look around that hes lost.
  B Corey finally admits (after taking time to look around) that he's lost.
  C Corey (finally admits) after taking time to look around that hes' lost.
  D Corey finally admits after taking time (to look around) that he'is lost.

3 Which sentence is written correctly?

  A Please wash (my shirt) the blue one and (my pants) the green ones.
  B Please wash (my shirt the blue one) and (my pants the green ones).
  C Please wash my shirt (the blue one) and my pants (the green ones).
  D Please wash my shirt the (blue) one and my pants the (green) ones.

4 Which sentence is written correctly?

  A Mannys coat i'snt in the closet.
  B Manny's coat isnt' in the closet.
  C Manny's coat isn't in the closet.
  D Mannies coat is'nt in the closet.

Go On

Language Arts
© Houghton Mifflin Harcourt Publishing Company. All rights reserved.

Grade 5, Unit 6: Journey to Discovery

Name _____   Date _____

Lesson 30
WEEKLY TESTS 30.10

**Get Lost!
The Puzzle of Mazes**
Language Arts

5 Which sentence is written correctly?

   A I have the following requests' put your toys away, make your bed, and put your clean clothes in the dresser.
   B I have the following requests: put your toys away, make your bed, and put your clean clothes in the dresser.
   C I have the following requests, put your toys away, make your bed, and put your clean clothes in the dresser.
   D I have the following requests; put your toys away, make your bed, and put your clean clothes in the dresser.

6 Which sentence is written correctly?

   A The bus stopped at Marthas house at 3;30 P.M.
   B The bus stopped at Marthas' house at 3,30 P.M.
   C The bus stopped at Martha's house at 3:30 P.M.
   D The bus' stopped at Marthas house at 3(30) P.M.

7 Which sentence is written correctly?

   A Amy's (friend Tonya) lives near (Mr. Wilsons market) on Starlight Road.
   B Amy's friend (Tonya) lives near Mr. Wilson's market (on Starlight Road).
   C Amys friend (Tonya) lives near Mr. Wilson's (market on Starlight Road).
   D Amys' (friend) Tonya lives near Mr. Wilsons' market on (Starlight Road).

8 Which sentence is written correctly?

   A Youre looking for Dads key's in the wrong place.
   B You're looking for Dads' keys in the wrong place.
   C Youre looking for Dad's key's in the wrong place.
   D You're looking for Dad's keys in the wrong place.

Language Arts

Grade 5, Unit 6: Journey to Discovery

Name _____ Date _____

Lesson 30
WEEKLY TESTS 30.11

**Get Lost!
The Puzzle of Mazes**
Language Arts

9 Which sentence is written correctly?

  A Tyrone didn't have time to go to the library today, so he'll have to go tomorrow.
  B Tyrone did'nt have time to go to the library today, so he'll have to go tomorrow.
  C Tyrone didnt' have time to go to the library today, so h'ell have to go tomorrow.
  D Tyrone didnt have time to go to the library today, so he'll have to go tomorrow.

10 Which sentence is written correctly?

  A Lets see if Pam's alarm rings at 6.30 A.M.
  B Lets see if Pams' alarm ring's at 6:30 A.M.
  C Lets' see if Pams alarm rings' at 6;30 A.M.
  D Let's see if Pam's alarm rings at 6:30 A.M.

STOP

Language Arts
© Houghton Mifflin Harcourt Publishing Company. All rights reserved.

Grade 5, Unit 6: Journey to Discovery